T0328347

Healing or Stealing?

Jean-Marie Abgrall

Healing or Stealing?

—

Medical Charlatans in the New Age

Algora Publishing
New York

Algora Publishing, New York
© 2001 by Algora Publishing
All rights reserved. Published 2001.
Printed in the United States of America
ISBN: 1-892941-51-1
Editors@algora.com

Originally published as *Les charlatans de la santé*, © Éditions Payot
et Rivages, 1998
Library of Congress Cataloging-in-Publication Data 00-011923

Abgrall, Jean-Marie.
  [Charlatans de la santé. English]
  Healing or stealing : medical charlatans in the new age / by
Jean-Marie Abgrall.
    p. ; cm.
  ISBN 1-892941-51-1 (alk. paper)
  1. Alternative medicine. 2. Quacks and quackery.
  [DNLM: 1. Alternative Medicine. 2. Quackery. WB 890 A147c 2000a]
I. Title.
  R733 .A24513 2000
  615.8'56—dc21

                          00-011923

Front Cover: *Dr. Mayer-Hermann* by Otto Dix (1926)

Algora Publishing
wishes to express appreciation
to the French Ministry of Culture
for its support
of this work through the
Centre National du livre

New York
www.algora.com

Table of Contents

INTRODUCTION

After my last book was published — *Soul Snatchers: The Mechanics of Cults**— I received an avalanche of letters with specific questions or asking me to shed some light on writers' personal quests that had "turned out badly", leading to an experience with cults. This correspondence brought me great quantities of new information on various aspects of the cult phenomenon, particularly in France and Europe.

Reviewing all these cases, from many countries, I could not help noticing that one of the principal avenues used by cults, one of their best lures and selling points, was "patamedicine". (I have coined this term on the basis of Alfred Jarry's "pataphysics", meaning the *science of imaginary solutions*, a term that was also borrowed by Prof. Marcel Francis Kahn.) Well-being seminars, symposiums on nontraditional medicine, and alternative medicine treatment centers, together with palm-readers, séances, and esoteric conferences, form a rich compost. The cults of healing flourish in this fertile matrix, along with prayer groups and healers of every ilk.

Certainly, not every practitioner of alternative (or natural) medi-

*English edition by Algora Publishing, 1999.

cine is a cult recruiter, but the daily battle they wage against rationality helps to widen the breach in the wall of doubt that separates suffering individuals from ecstatic fools — devout believers in the revelation of healing.

Taking my observations a little further, I was compelled to note that some of my fellow professionals (some in good faith, some not) were propagating ideas that are contrary to the minimum level of rationality necessary to avoid the traps presented by all the ideological inclinations of our end-of-millennium society. The problem is so immense that the French National Order of Physicians has addressed it on several occasions, weighing in with opinions or publishing recommendations, generally to no avail.

Lastly, confronted with critical cases that made headlines in the legal, forensic and mass media (The Order of the Solar Temple, for example), I saw how many potentially dangerous social groups — coercive cults, apocalyptic groups — recruited many of their followers in doctors' offices. Patients go in, looking for a treatment that is "less aggressive" than traditional medicine, and find themselves being initiated into the enlightened program of a group that may well lead them to the intensive care unit, if not to the morgue.

Having digested all this information, I was faced with a simple choice: to keep quiet in order to avoid running up against public sensitivities, or to denounce, loud and clear, how the world of "care-giving" was going astray. Keeping quiet when one knows so much can only be considered complicity; and in the present case it would amount to failure to report a crime (or at least a misdemeanor), or even failure to come to the assistance of someone in danger — which is itself a crime, in France. It is hard to know where to point one's finger. Who is to blame for this deviance — doctors, aides, healers, quacks, charlatans? Where do we draw the line? The difference is slim between practitioners of good faith and crooks, between those who "believe" in their daily practice and those who are cynical con artists.

4

Even if one believes that homeopathy, as such, is not harmful, it is still true that the time the patient spends pursuing such remedies is definitively wasted, which means that he has less chance of finding a real cure, especially since certain "fundamentalist" therapists willfully divert the patient from so-called traditional medicine. Similarly, while acupuncture cannot worsen a patient's condition (if the rules of asepsis are respected), it can delay a proper diagnosis and treatment. Lastly, while osteopathy practiced by a doctor or a qualified physical therapist is a valuable tool, the same technique employed by a self-proclaimed therapist who has only a superficial knowledge of anatomy can result in permanent quadriplegia. As for the various charlatans of healthcare, they are not satisfied to make pronouncements (the word charlatan comes from Italian *ciarlare*, "to talk emphatically"), they very often divert patients from what may be their only chances of survival.

I wrote this book to try to draw the attention of healthcare consumers to the risks that are born whenever we entrust ourselves to any individual whom we assume possesses a new knowledge, a new technique, or even a new wisdom. "Mainstream" medicine certainly has its weakness and its swindlers, but it behaves like a self-regulating organism and the errors of the few are very often (not always) compensated by the devotion and the knowledge of the others. Overall, its performance has been "generally good", even if errors sometimes cause a stir the forensic world and become top news stories.

For several decades, now, the medical consumer has been making an effort to analyze and distinguish what is useful in this field, and what is nonsense. He has tried to separate the wheat from the chaff, but he is kept in a state of doubt by magazines and special interest groups that profit by disseminating methods that at best are nutty, and at worst are fatal.

In seeking to analyze the phenomenon of patamedicine, I thought in all good faith that I would be able to explain this trend and to come up with useful theories as to what has caused it. But the further I go, the more I discover wild new fantasies, new gadgets, and new scams. Some of these techniques come from historical sources, theories or instigators; others were born of the delusion of a pseudo-enlightened individual, a pseudo-Messiah or a pure crook.

This book sometimes looks like a laundry list, or the inventory of an imaginary home improvement store with aisles full of instruments to fix every conceivable problem. I have given many examples in this odd bazaar, but lacking the energy to write several volumes, I had to leave out innumerable practices that are quite as fraudulent as those that I denounce here.

Without wishing to create a cheap work of exaggerated rationalism, I wanted to erect a bulwark against the irrational that is parasiting our society. This book is not intended as an act of hostility against all the practitioners of alternative medicines, against all those who have taken to heart the old proverb *"primum non nocere"*, against all those who provide care and comfort. But it is so intended against those who thrive on disease and suffering, and who take advantage of them by exploiting human credulity and everyone's desire to live. Seneca wrote: "He who does not prevent a crime, when he can, encourages it" (*The Trojans*).

1. FROM ALTERNATIVE MEDICINE TO PATAMEDICINE

Pataphysics is the science of imaginary solutions. It symbolically ascribes to the depiction of an object the same properties held by the object itself.

Alfred Jarry.

No one is more positive than the pataphysician, determined to place everything on the same level; he is ready to receive and accept everything with equal enthusiasm.

Dr. I. L. Sandonien,
College of Pataphysics.

Alternative medicine has become widely accepted today. In France alone, some 60,000 non-doctor therapists (hypnotists, clairvoyants, osteopaths) staff this army for medical misinformation. Thanks to the increasing legal and economic unification of Europe and the harmonization of the countries' legislations, as well as of the resulting practices, there are nearly 40,000 "illegal therapists" who are trying to acquire recognized status as health experts or health aides, generally without any sound basis.

The number of doctors whose practices were established according to normal rules but who also practice alternative medicine is harder to measure, because the bodies responsible for oversight do not recognize disciplines such as homeopathy, osteopathy, iridology[1], trichology[2] or auriculo-therapy. However, there is reason to believe that nearly 10% of them practice these unrecognized disciplines either exclusively or in conjunction with other treatments.

Given the extent of the phenomenon, in 1982, the (French) Ministry of Health named Dr. J. H. Niboyet to prepare a report on the forms of health care that are not governed by an educational or training program administered at the national level. On the basis of that report, in 1983, the Conference of the Deans of Medical Colleges raised the question of possibly coming up with an official instruction program on homeopathy and acupuncture. It should be noted that since 1982, under the impetus of Professor Cornillot, Dean of the Faculty of Medicine at Bobigny, seven of these therapies (acupuncture, homeopathy, auriculotherapy, osteopathy, phyto-therapy, meso-therapy, and trace elements) received a preliminary official legitimization in the context of that university. Nearly 1500 students, for the most part doctors who were already practicing, are currently studying for university diplomas in natural medicine.

The Academy of Medicine takes a contrary attitude toward alternative therapies, as Professors Gounelle de Pontanel and Tuchmann-Duplessis reminded us in a 1984 press release: "Given the state of the science today, the prescription of homeopathic remedies is not an act of reason but remains an act of faith as long as the scientific bases of its effectiveness have not been established." And Gounelle de Pontanel added, ironically: "Will we find ourselves, tomorrow, planning to give official recognition to the divining rod as a diagnostic means equal to the stethoscope, and the laying on of hands as a therapeutic procedure?" Professor Sournia, likewise a member of the Academy of Medicine, recently wrote that alternative medicine is a "regression", a return to a "pre-scientific era of humanity".[3]

On February 26, 1985, at the request of President Mitterrand, the Minister for Social Affairs and the Health Secretary commissioned a new study on the "development of unconventional medical techniques known as alternative or natural medicines". The conclusions of this report, ambiguous as it may have been, did not quite produce the kind of resounding echoes looked for by the adherents of "patamedicine". I should specify that the "Study Group on Alternative Medicines" was flawed in its composition, and this in itself predicted its possible rec-ommendations:

> Doesn't assigning such an evaluation to a group dominated by cancer specialists necessarily restrict the field of investigation to "non-proven" methods against cancer? And furthermore, the fact is that at least three of the four selected members . . . are practitioners of the medicines under study. Does such a composition allow the proper conditions, including the irenism, necessary for research[4]?

The 1985 report offered a warning, in its conclusions on the valid-ity of "alternative medicines"; and it emphasized, rightly, the economic aspect, which is the principal argument that favors the burgeoning de-velopment of these uncertain therapies. Homeopathy laboratories' an-nual sales quintupled between 1979 and 1985 and have more than dou-bled since then. By 1998, the figure was nearing $250 million per an-num, in France alone. And consumption of medicinal plants represents a significant commercial sector in terms of marketing as well as pro-duction and processing.

On the other hand, most of the products on the market are not reimbursable via the usual insurance plans. When they are reimbursed, the cost to the insurer (for example, for homeopathic capsules) is far lower than that of the new formulas originating from pharmaceutical research. It goes without saying that homeopathic starch or sugar granules do not entail high production costs and that, for the laborato-ries, these are only profitable if they are sold in large quantity. French homeopathic laboratories, by the way, are the top exporters in the world, in this sector.

These economic arguments may partly explain the lack of enthusi-asm of the public administration for establishing more control over what can be seen as the equivalent of a series of booby traps for the gul-lible. They find a favorable echo among adherents of alternative medi-cines — and among those who make a living off them.

Indeed, it is easy to underscore the difference between the "apparent" social cost of "natural" prescriptions and that of allopathic prescriptions. However, the calculation does not take account of the lost days of activity, and the cost of complications and even mortality related to the use of these supposed medications. And yet, we are being culturally brainwashed, with the aim of making us accept that patamedicine has a useful role to play.

Today the designation "nontraditional medicine" seems to be retained only for the major diseases (cancer, AIDS). In this context, the concept of "non-traditionalism" implies abandoning "traditional" medicine in favor of patamedicine. The expression "nontraditional medicine" is gradually ceding ground to terms such as "less aggressive treatment" and "natural" and "alternative medicine", which create the illusion that it is not necessary to abandon "traditional" medicine and that there can be complementarity, even synergy, between medicine and patamedicine. The term "alternative" implies the possibility of choice on the part of the patient. The term "nontraditional" has a more political connotation, as an "antidote" to "traditional" medicine; it is a reflection of our consumer society, offering a less expensive form of treatment that is supposedly of high quality and is, in theory, accessible to all (and therefore, to the less well-to-do). This political undertone is an extension of a line of thought that pervades books like those by Ivan Illich[5], but this thinking was picked up by the pataphysicians and its original meaning has been distorted. The term "less aggressive" suggests the same symbolism as that of "natural", but with the added connotation of pejorative judgment on traditional medicine, which is seen as "harsh" and "aggressive".

Here we find a dichotomy that is encouraged by consumer protection trends that impinge on the medical field, among others. Being a more knowledgeable consumer, in terms of medicine or patamedicine, means preferring medicine that is "risk free", "natural" (in the sense of "closer to nature"), "inexpensive" (with the insinuation that it is accessible to everyone, including inhabitants of the Third and Fourth Worlds), as distinguished from a type of medicine that is "aggressive" (or based on chemistry or physics, products of a market economy), "artificial" (and thus polluting), and "expensive" (and thus reserved to the developed nations whose economies are devastating the planet).

Some of the arguments used by the advocates of patamedicine are judicious and it is true that our Western society at the down of the new millennium has not done a great job of managing the gains in medical achievement. The economic stakes often take precedence over the patients' interests; many invented formulas are put on the market without sufficient study; and finally, the pharmaceutical companies generally prefer marketing over scientific proof. Even so, must we reject all rationality and place our health, and sometimes our lives, in the hands of the healers, alchemists, sibyls and soothsayers of the modern world?

What's Causing the Fad?

For the last 25 years, the psychology of the patient/consumer has been evolving, and at the same time his sense of belonging to a specific social group has diminished. While the first half of the 20th century witnessed the establishment of the great social protection programs and gradually integrated the citizen into a health care system related to his economic station (individual plans, trade union plans, etc.), the 1980's by contrast witnessed the breakdown of the system in many countries. The "social" security system gave way to "illness" insurance — and budgetary considerations took precedence over health requirements. The social fabric unraveled, leaving the citizen/patient to his own devices, pondering in relative isolation how best to "come to terms" with the system.

So-called traditional medicine was suspect, because of its ambiguous relations with the pharmaceutical "producers", because of its elite status and its retrograde attitudes (concerning abortion, for example), but especially because of the loss of the doctor-patient bond which had been the basis of the care-giving relationship. Changing morals and the new constraints that weigh upon the individual led people to give themselves a new sense of freedom by opening up to the choice of non-traditional healthcare practices. Over the course of time, the two-way bond between patient and doctor was weakened, damaged by the third-party payment system (insurance), which ends up controlling the patient, the doctor and the care that is provided. The failure of contractual and friendly policies has led to increasingly heavy-handed state intervention to the detriment of the doctor-patient partnership, which has split into two parties with sometimes antinomical interests. Access to the best care (often the most recent, sometimes the most expensive) does not necessarily agree with budgetary considerations. Faced with growing constraints, the patient tends to escape more and more often toward the arenas of medical freedom that the "non-traditional" practitioners represent, and this with the blessing of the public organizations and insurance companies who are, for the time being, discharged from the responsibility of paying for certain procedures.

"Nontraditional" medicine is first and foremost a freeform medicine wherein the patient agrees to assume the cost of his care, without counting on "coverage", and wherein the practitioner, freed from public and professional supervision, can prescribe and practice examinations and treatments however he wishes — and the fewer ties he has with the establishment, the more freely he can practice. The conventional doctor is more constrained than the unconventional one, who in turn is more constrained than the practitioner who is not a doctor at all. As the level of social and professional freedom increases, the prescribed "therapy" has less need to abide by any rule. The increase in anomalous practices is accompanied by a decrease in technical skills and expertise, which are reduced proportionally. Only the supreme control of criminal law remains, which often proves unable to tell the difference between sensible practices and scams, for lack of laws governing "patamedicine".

Released from the medical-insurance yoke, the patient finds alternative medicines all the more attractive since their spiel generally takes a global view of the individual himself, and then of the individual in society, and finally of the individual in the cosmos — an approach that permits talk loaded with philosophical, political, even moralistic connotations. The patient is presented as responsible for his own actions and thus for his disease, but also as a victim of a social system that produces pathologies. The mechanistic aspect of the traditional medical approach is replaced by language whose orientation corresponds to the subject's unacknowledged instincts and propensities. Now the patient can "live naturally, free, without constraints, becoming master of his own destiny, by seeing his acts in the context of a cosmic destiny".

Moreover, choosing nontraditional medicine permits the subject to make adjustments and to take a graduated response to his pathology. "Less-aggressive" medicine is in theory the answer for "less-aggressive" diseases. If the pathology worsens, this can be supplemented with traditional medicine. Nontraditional medicine takes the lead if traditional medicine is failing and the prognosis looks grim. Thus, many practitioners of alternative medicine avoid the risk of having the validity of their treatment put to the test. Most pathologies thus treated are "self-curing" without resorting to any therapy whatsoever — and alternative medicine generally plays the part of a placebo drug.

When it is coupled with traditional medicine, alternative medicine only interferes with the real care. It becomes a waste of time for the rational practitioner, who finds himself having to explain why, in spite of the 30 H C Perlimpinpinus pills prescribed by the pataphysician, one must also take antibiotics. The real problems surface when, under the pretext of freedom of choice, patients afflicted with serious illnesses refuse traditional medicine outright, choosing to trust in a charlatan of nontraditional medicine instead. This is happening more and more frequently, since traditional medicine is sometimes powerless or too slow to deal with severe pathologies. In fact, patamedicines of all kinds are generally addressed to two audiences: individuals who do not need any care at all, and those whose pathology is sufficiently grave to present a dire prognosis which, as a side effect, saps the credibility of traditional medicine.

The Arguments of Official Medicine and of Alternative Medicines

The reports of the study groups reflecting on alternative medicines accurately highlight the arguments of both sides. It is not very likely that the "official" arguments can convince those who believe in alternative medicines, and yet they to appear to be founded on common sense:

- Medicine should accept only those therapies that have been proven effective and harmless;
- This harmlessness and this effectiveness must be proven by experience and experimentation;
- Such tests are incompatible with the mystery that is maintained around certain practices and the metaphysical-religious character of others;
- The "alternative" practitioner must not shelter behind a "secret"; he must prove — if not explain — the effectiveness of his nontraditional procedures.

The 1985 report summarized these reservations:

One of the greatest dangers that alternative or unproven medicines present to the patient is that they can persuade him that they are generally harmless, even if they may not always be effective. Then there is the great risk that before a proven course of treatment is begun, patients afflicted with serious illnesses will waste precious time that can never be regained; this wasted time, during which the patient's condition will worsen, must be accounted as a pathogenic effect of these forms of "medicine".

Ultimately, the following opinion, the most generally accepted in the realm of "official" medicine, concisely summarizes these various arguments: alternative medicine encompasses a range of practices that have never truly been proven reliable. Given the current state of our knowledge, one could tolerate these practices as long as they do not claim to apply to grave illnesses, thus making the patient miss other chances of being cured. Still, something has to be done to address the problem, taking into account the current situation.

The success these forms of medicine enjoy in public opinion is easily explained by the French taste for the paradoxical, for the weird, for everything that seems to be opposed to the established order, and by the fairly favorable treatment they receive in certain of the media. But serious-minded people should make no mistake: the few elements of value must be distinguished from the hot air and the mystification, all of which are carefully combined with powers of suggestion that are likely to bring into play the placebo effect that is so difficult to eliminate from any rigorously and scientifically controlled therapeutic evaluation.

In contrast, alternative medicines reproach traditional medicine on the following grounds:
- Official medicine is not interested in new techniques.

While that is sometimes true initially, there is no known case in which it was not suggested that the "revolutionary" practitioner submit proof. But, unfortunately, this suggestion seldom meets a response adequate to the needs of medical care (ex: the Beljanski scandal[6]).
- Official medicine is often obscurantist.

Recent history reminds us that Roentgen and his disciples did overcome the refusal to recognize the reality of X-rays, in spite of the opposition of the "Faculty". Actually, current practice is based more and more on fundamental research, followed by applied research, provided the usual protocols are respected that govern the evolution of a theory into a therapeutic application.

- Official medicine cannot explain all the effects of the products it employs.

Indeed, even today nobody can explain how products like aspirin work. But the proof of their effectiveness can be seen every day in experimental protocols carried out *in vitro* as well as *in vivo*, on man as well as on animals.

- Alternative medicine's strongest argument against official medicine is that it treats the patient only in terms of the symptom and not in relation to his own identity and his condition as a social individual.

This charge is justified, as simple observation of current practices shows. But even if the doctor gradually loses his feel for his patients, even if specialization leads to the patient being perceived only in terms of "systems" and not in terms of the "ensemble", does that mean that we should permit every kind of pseudo-medical act under the pretext that it addresses the entire individual?

I happened to examine a young mother who was stricken with breast cancer. Under the influence of her "Masters" in alternative medicine, she had chosen a form of care intended to save her cosmic entity. She had refused radiation therapy on the advice of practitioners who claimed to be "mechanistic". According to them, radiation treatments would make holes in her etheric body. I can easily summarize the cosmic result of her choice: the human mechanism was unable to withstand the recommended purification fast, and our planet inherited two additional orphans.

All hypocritical and demagogic patter notwithstanding, the fundamental principle of any *real* medicine is and must remain: *Curare et primum non nocere* ("To heal, and above all not to harm"). All harmful practices must be fought and condemned outright, even if that means incurring the wrath of some part of the *vox populi*, who are kept in the dark by a form of obscurantism that favors certain special interest groups.

Who are the Victims of Alternative Medicines?

On the basis of market research conducted by the media that specialize in natural medicine, we can provide the outlines of the robot-portrait of those who use patamedicine.

The population in question is almost entirely female, middle-aged (35 to 50 years old), and includes senior managers and professionals, members of the middle class, and ordinary employees. Laborers and farmers generally place their confidence in official medicine. With the exception of patients of healers and bonesetters, who are located in rural areas, most of this population resides in medium- to large-sized towns and cities. There are basically two types of consumers: on the one hand, those who only resort to alternative medicines as an exception, and for whom they are an auxiliary therapy; and those who rely on them systematically. The latter approach becomes part of a kind of cosmogonic re-tooling, with a vision of a mission to be achieved or an enhanced lifestyle to be realized. The use of alternative medicines often goes hand in hand with a spiritual or religious quest, which explains the importance of "ritual" in these forms of medicine.

The people who turn to these therapies are, in descending order:

- patients suffering from chronic disorders whose origin and cause cannot be pinpointed — what are called "functional disorders" (insomnia, headaches, fatigue, digestive disorders, allergies, and "ideopathic" hypertension);
- patients presenting acute, but not very grave, symptoms;
- people who use these therapies preventively, for maintenance, in order to "stay healthy";

- people who choose to undergo a detoxification process (for smoking, drug addiction, alcoholism, excessive eating);
- and, finally, cases that are considered "incurable", i.e. cases that official medicine has given up as hopeless and for whom alternative therapies are the last resort[7].

However, "recruitment" to alternative medicine presupposes a particular psychological profile, mainly with regard to the person's relation to the external world. The "alternative medicine" culture has enjoyed a revival that goes hand in hand with the New Age explosion. While some practices are anchored in the past (magnetism, dowsing, healers, etc.), others, on the contrary, are more a sign of protest or opposition to the social standards adopted by the so-called consumer society.

This dynamic, which is a form of rebellion against the ruling authorities, is fed by the advent of the "myth of the clean" (as opposed to the nuclear, and to various other types of pollution). The individual seeks to take greater charge of his own body and to remove it from the actions that have become standard within the group. Rejecting imposed health practices amounts to a kind of return to the origin, and to the Earth Mother. The growth of environmentalism, the primary form of ecologist thinking, is one of the vehicles of this new expansion.

Cultural contributions from all sides (Hopi Indian, Tibetan, aboriginal. . .), simmered together in a New Age sauce, have given rise to a multitude of new (but supposedly traditional) techniques based on research on the primitive state — Rousseau's "good savage", the Garden of Eden, etc.. New medicines are used to "re-enchant" the world and to return it to the natural state, as social psychologist Serge Moscovici says, by releasing it from the grime of industrialization.

Treating the Person or Treating the Symptoms? Origins of Holistic Medicine

The frank opposition between traditional medicine and patamedicine is built on the patients' desire to avoid having their relationships to their therapists become mechanical. Alternative medicine enthusiasts like to describe traditional medicine as a technique that is interested only in the symptom, seldom in the real cause, and never in the individual *in totum*. A quick look at the evolution of the profession over the past fifty years shows that medicine has undergone mutations that naturally flow from technical progress — and the subsequent questioning of technical progress — and that coincide with society's development as a whole, mainly by confronting the concept of total care.

The general practitioner had been losing ground to a kind of "hard core" technocrat, but the increased expense and patients' complaints caused a reaction that has led to a gradual restoration of the "traditional" doctor's prestige to the detriment of the technical wizards of medicine. However, medicine is not monolithic: the last of the family doctors practice side-by-side with the super-technicians of the teaching hospitals and old-fashioned doctors commingle with those who are obsessed with scanners.

At any event, in response to the distress of patients who were no longer willing to be regarded as machines in need of repair, the pata-physicians jumped to fill the deserted relational niche. Mitigating their technical insufficiency or outright incompetence with increased listening skills, they found a ready market in the health field, and they used sales pitches that are far superior to the actual products offered. Thus pata-medical marketing has little by little replaced the benevolent ear of the official doctor.

The concept of overall care for the patient was reintroduced by "holistic" medicine, when official medicine was getting mired in an exogenic approach to disease. Historically, Pasteur's identification of the microbial agent's importance in infection caused an abrupt shift in our understanding of the causative factors of the pathological phenomenon. For centuries, medicine had been dominated by the concept of phenomena "internal to the body". The theory of humors was the perfect illustration. It held that disease corresponds to an excess or deficiency of the four fundamental humors: heat, cold, dryness, humidity (fever being a disorder of the humor of heat, aneurisms a disorder relating to dryness, etc.). The Pasteurian revolution moved the cause of disease from something internal to the body to something external to the body, and it did it so sharply that the concept of the patient's responsibility for his disease was little by little erased.

However, while it is true that one may be predisposed to a particular disease, it cannot be denied that the subject does have some personal control over the disease — for example, by observing hygienic and dietary rules. Health and disease are, in fact, the result of causes both internal and external, independent of the will of the patient but quite likely to be affected by his actions and behaviors.

The external view of causality, the latest interpretation of the genesis and treatment of disease, has put the patient in a position of total dependence on the doctor. Placed in the hands of "the one who knows best", the patient no longer has any room to act or to choose, pinned between the external aggression of the disease, on the one hand, and the assistance of medical knowledge on the other.

In response to this caricature of the patient buffeted by the waves of both the disease and of medicine, "less aggressive" medicines have breathed new life into the medical past, resuscitating it with the breath of the New Age — and primacy has once again been granted to the endogenous concept of disease. For the New Ager, disease is still the result of some form of aggression, but an aggression that has found fertile ground on which it could develop its harmful effects. Alternative medicines have brought back into style the old concepts of temperament, biological or astrological type, capacity of self-defense, characterology, morpho-psychology and, today, of bio-morpho-genealogy.

With reason, but also with an acute sense for medical marketing, alternative medicines have offered the patient a new vision of her status. The technician's approach, which regards the patient as a human mechanism made up of parts to be repaired, has been supplanted by a new emphasis on the individual as a whole, perceived as a unique entity that has been shaped by her immediate or remote environment. Disease is presented as a disturbance in the balance between the person and herself, the person and her surroundings, or between the person and the cosmos.

The patient's sensitivity thus leads her toward the alternative approaches and guides her choice of "treatment". For those who want to find a place within tradition, theories such as those of fluids, temperaments, and characters explain the lack of harmony with oneself; ecologicial sensibilities will be attracted by the theories of agressology and rupture with the environment; as for those who thirst for a sense of the absolute, they will be if not cured then at least reassured by the cosmic vision of their disease.

With the New Age, the concept of *holistic* medicine (a term coined out of the Greek word "holos", "the whole", together with the English "holy") has enjoyed a surge of renewed interest from the general public and the consumer market in the United States. Holistic medicine (or holism) had already had its hour of glory in Europe between the two world wars. In 1920-1930, French holism, led by the psychoanalyst and homeopath Réné Allendy, sought to respond to the inadequacies of Pasteurian medicine by trying to amalgamate into the one all-embracing theoretical construct such marginal therapies as iridology, osteopathy, central-therapy[8] or homeopathy. This global approach took the name of *synthetic* medicine.

Allendy and his confreres based their approach on an acknowledgement that the medicine of the time was failing, dominated as it was by a proliferation of laboratory tests that "fragmented" the clinical approach to the patient. Like holistic medicine today, synthetic medicine tended to recycle the ensemble of therapeutic practices that are not well-codified but are appreciated by the public.

From 1930 on, synthetic medicine underwent an evolution when its leaders adopted a political stance. The crisis of the inter-regnum period and the rise of various currents of Fascism in Europe led syn-thetic medicine to positions itself in political terms — as Ivan Illich did, with the New Age revival.

One current of synthetic medicine would congregate around an ideology dominated by the desire to retrieve the sacred values of French society and to promote the traditional family, to encourage social order and to purify the French race through eugenic practices. Another branch would, to some extent, embody the left of the holistic move-ment, which sees capitalism as the major obstacle to man's being con-sidered in all his corporal integrity and his social dimension.[9]

Both of these tendencies are found in the current holistic move-ment, which means that now the hardcore defenders of tradition are in the same boat with those who are concerned for man's condition as an individual. The two groups share a vitalistic conception of the human being. In holistic thought, the patient is considered in his totality; and he finds a sacred dimension to his terrestrial and cosmic destiny. Holis-tic medicine not only aims to treat the disease and look after the body but also to give meaning to life — not a meaning at the individual level, but indeed a "cosmic" meaning, which gives the human microcosm a place within the galactic macrocosm.

This philosophical-religious approach is not in itself condemna-ble, but one might wonder how much it has to do with being able to solve particular problems of ill-health. For members of the Order of the Solar Temple, a healthy body represented the vehicle necessary for cos-mic initiation. Thus, patients who found their way into homeopathy through Dr. Jouret or his codisciples were gradually brainwashed to the point of carrying out their great cosmic intention of departing for Sir-ius, the brightest star in the night sky, by burning themselves to death. As another sign of deviant beliefs, certain adherents of medical move-ments with religious overtones (the Grail, for instance) accept disease as an expression of their terrestrial karma, as a test to be undergone in order to attain divine unity, and they refuse the help of traditional medicine which they see as an expression of earthly sin.

The explosion of the New Age and a new form of everyday magic, the turmoil of the post-war era and the agonizing reassessments of a liberal economy that is reaching its limits, the demise of the autocratic ideologies of the 19th and the 20th centuries, the end of the millennium — which, for some, meant the end of the world — and the advent of new philosophical and religious paradigms, have all contributed to the haphazard construction of a body of thought that has taken hold among fringe groups. Patamedicine is a fertile field for its development.

A new public debate has begun, over the admissibility of certain practices. While an individual's choice of one charlatanesque practice or another cannot and should not be challenged, it is our duty to consider the consequences these practices have on society as a whole. This includes the economic burden caused by the aggravation of pathologies that went untreated and the need to treat the somatic, corporeal damage caused by aberrant techniques, but also the social consequences of the formation of parallel channels that are outside of any control or governing mechanism, and the criminological consequences of the existence of links between patamedicine and cults.

This new social and medical dynamics has two major branches. In one category are those deriving from historical patamedical pursuits (acupuncture, homeopathy, osteopathy), and in the other are the recent creations, born by spontaneous generation, that are used by individuals suffering from delusions or in the context of organized fraud (ovo-therapy, tele-therapy) — or that may be linked to a "tradition" but are little by little distinguishing themselves, through highly effective marketing campaigns (urine therapy).

2.   AND THEN CAME HAHNEMANN

They know, my brother, that which I have told you, they who do not cure much; and all the excellence of their art consists of pompous gibberish, and specious prattle, giving you words in place of reasons, and promises in place of effects.

Molière,

The Imaginary Invalid.

First place, in the list of supposedly therapeutic practices that can to lead charlatanism and to patamedicine, goes to homeopathy.[1] Many homeopaths are not out to get rich, nor to turn medicine into a farce, but homeopathy by its very bases represents a source of profit that is out of all proportion to its effectiveness. One has only to look at the annual revenue figures for the laboratories that supply this industry.[2]

Practiced with conscience and understanding, homeopathy is neither more nor less effective than the traditional array of placebos that flood the dietetic and cosmetic market: pills against ageing, hair loss, and fatigue, and for weight loss, enhanced sexuality, better school performance, etc.. Unfortunately, it also serves as a forum for many deviant practices and is used as a recruiting ground for many healers, for cults and for the founders of esoteric-medical movements.

If proof is needed, here is a piece of mail that I received from an eminent colleague who is a homeopath; all his life he has strived to have the practice of homeopathy carried out within the code of medical practice and the rules of the highest morals.

25

As a teacher of homeopathy and as author of *La Matière medical de référence*, I am "horrified" by the direction taken by some of my former students, which raises several questions for me. The presentation of which I am sending you a copy is intended mainly for a severely "contaminated" group of which I am about to assume the presidency. . . . I doubt very much that the homeopathic press, being distrustful and under pressure, will publish it, and I don't care.

This letter was addressed to me shortly after the headlines had been full of the tribulations of the Order of the Solar Temple and the homeopathic doctors associated with it, such as Dr. Jouret. The Grail Movement had also just been nailed, with two of its leaders arrested in the death of a disciple, due to lack of care.

However surprising it may seem, there are practitioners with high standards who still cannot admit that homeopathy bears within itself the seeds of its own devolution; they refuse to notice what simple common sense and a little scientific rigor make clear to any observer who stops to consider the terms of homeopathic action.

The Origins of Homeopathy

While homeopaths sometimes claim to be followers of Hippocrates, the founder of the homeopathic doctrines and practice is Samuel Hahnemann (1755-1843). A German doctor who had partially given up his medical practice in 1790 in order to devote himself to translation work, he came to notice that the bark of quinine had certain peculiar effects had when he consumed it. Having ingested 12.6 grams of bark of quinine twice a day over a period of several days, when he was in good health, he noted that he began to exhibit most of the symptoms of "intermittent" fever (malaria), the condition that quinine was usually prescribed to combat.

On the strength of this observation, he then set to work to study systematically the effects of various plants and chemicals, on himself and his disciples: arsenic, belladonna, digitalis, walnut, broad beans and others. Hahnemann and his disciples then conscientiously noted the various symptoms induced by the products introduced, and looked for similarities to the symptoms observed during well-known illnesses. Quinine seemed to induce the clinical signs of malaria: coldness of the extremities, heart palpitations, tremors, headaches, mental fogginess and thirst.

But curiously, Hahnemann and his disciples, from the very inception of their observations, showed a general tendency to ignore certain of the symptoms when they were absent or were inconsistent. Thus, Hahnemann noted himself that after taking quinine he "did not feel that particular shiver of the pernicious attack". From the start, the dice were loaded, since the principal symptom, the fever, is "forgotten" in the statement of the criteria shared by malaria and the signs of intoxication by quinine.

Nevertheless Hahnemann derived the guiding principle of homeopathy from these supposed concordances: the *"law of similarity"*, expressed by the Latin proverb *Similia similibus curantur* ("like cures like"). In the course of the experiments, Hahnemann established a catalogue of the concordances between products and maladies.

But he soon ran into a major stumbling block: the relative toxicity of the products in question. Thus, while one may absorb quinine at the price of some merely unpleasant symptoms, the same cannot be said for poisons such as arsenic, mercury, aconite or strychnine.

The technical impossibility of testing all the products whose effects are likely to compare with existing pathologies led to the articulation of the second great principle of homeopathy — which marked the beginning of the "compromises" of science to the benefit of obscurantism: *the principle of dilution*. Hahnemann imagined, in all logic, that he could dilute highly toxic products in order to be able to use them safely. Unfortunately, the diluted products suffer from one major defect: they do not cure, and neither do they induce secondary disorders. To deal with this "anomaly" in his reasoning and his assumptions, Hahnemann digressed from the scientific path that he had followed until that point, and adopted a quasi-magical attitude. He posited that diluting a product many times over not only does not diminish the therapeutic effect but multiplies it, at the same time eliminating the undesirable secondary effects.

However, even casual observation shows that the more a product is diluted, the less effective it is in its normal use. Hahnemann passed that hurdle by inventing the principle of the "dynamization" of the products. The basic commodity should not simply be diluted, it must be diluted according to a particular protocol that includes, at every stage of dilution, agitation by powerful shaking to "dynamize" the product. This protocol was named "succussions", and it became a ritual practice that magifies reality. Chemistry becomes alchemy.

The manufacturing technique is codified. One part of the active ingredient must be mixed with 99 parts of solvent, then subjected to a series of succussions. The product thus obtained from the first dilution (1 H C) is mixed in the same proportion (1:99) with the solvent, then dynamized, and the second centesimal dilution (2 H C) is obtained. In this way one can go up on to reach high dilutions, up to 30 H C.

Hahnemann had no difficulty convincing himself that the solvents used in all this manipulation were in and of themselves inert with respect to the diluted product. Thus alcohol, as a solvent, is "denied" as an active ingredient, as is lactose or starch used in making pills and homeopathic powders. The protocol for extracting the basic commodity itself sometimes takes surrealist forms. Thus, *Apis mellifica* (or bee venom) is extracted from dried, whole bees, but the bee must be provoked just before its death so that its venom is more powerful. Hahnemann did not specify whether it was necessary to stimulate spiders to obtain a stronger extract of Tarantula.

Coming on top of the law of similarity and that of dilution, the law of dynamization lodges homeopathy firmly in the realm of magic, leaving the field of science for that of the rabbit's foot and the four-leaf clover. Spelling out his theory, Hahnemann posits the principle that every therapy must be adapted to the patient, that there is no standard remedy for a standard patient and that every treatment must be selected according to a list of criteria that to some extent "explain" the patient. Since each patient has a unique identity, the homeopath does not describe a disease, he describes symptoms and an individual. It is the convergence of the symptoms and the type of individual that determines what should be prescribed. The medicine thus varies not only according to the symptoms (which would follow a certain logic) but according to equally important criteria that may be as different as the eye or hair color, body size and shape, sex, and temperament (carbonic, phosphoric, fluoric). Reliance on criteria like these when prescribing treatments has allowed the reintroduction today of abhorrent pursuits that really do not seem out of place the homeopathic galaxy: morpho-psychology, astrology and numerology.

In 1810, Hahnemann happily published the homeopathic bible, *The Organon of the Art of Healing*, and declared: "I recognize as disciples only those who practice pure homeopathy and whose treatments are entirely free of any combination with those means that had been employed up until now by the old medicine."

Hahnemann's scathing view of official medicine has been moderated by his later followers, but it did provoke traditional medicine's rejection of homeopathy, and this rejection persists to our day. In October 1984, the Academy of Medicine declared that it was "inappropriate, given the current state of knowledge, for the Colleges of Medicine and Pharmacy to grant diplomas certifying therapies that are neither accepted nor used by most of the medical profession". This declaration came on the heels of a recommendation by the National Council of the Order of Physicians demanding that alternative medicines "be tested according to criteria as severe as those to which the traditional diagnostic and therapeutic methods are subjected".

But after the European Parliament voted in 1992 to approve a recommendation to introduce homeopathy into the university curricula, these fine resolutions evaporated. On December 15, 1997, the National Council of the Order of Physicians publicized a study produced by its committee on homeopathy. The report's conclusions immediately elicited strong, mixed reactions from the medical profession, due to the timid wording adopted by the committee. Their conclusions make it clear that the committee members had conflicting opinions on the value of homeopathy. Even while the committee questioned its value, and recommended that the practice should be evaluated, they qualified it nevertheless as a therapy, and in lyrical terms — to the great satisfaction of its proselytes. Ideological lobbying had effectively taken over for industrial lobbying, and homeopathy — having achieved broad acceptability despite the protests — has created a precedent for charlatanesque practices, thus threatening the reliability of the medical profession.

Since then, it is easier to understand why the Order of Physicians does not try to set straight expert hucksters like Dr. G., who was quoted in the magazine *Science and Life* [*Science et vie*]: "Diseases are not caused by germs, nor viruses, nor bacteria, nor even virulent poisons at the biochemical level, but by their intimate nature, their vital force, their particular essence." Hahnemann's attempts at scientific rationalization have definitively given way to cosmic-energy doctrines, and magical thought has eliminated rational thought. The same Dr. G. declares that "the homeopathic practice is a constant inquiry into the bonds that link man with the cosmos, an exploration of the continuum that seems to exist between matter and consciousness".[3]

What's Wrong with Homeopathy?

The principle of similarity may not, in itself, deserve savage scientific opposition, even given Hahnemann's fundamental approximations;

the same cannot be said of the techniques of dilution and "succussion".

The principle of Hahnemann Concentrations establishes a formula for diluting a given product. With 1 H C (a one-hundredth Hahnemann dilution) we have one part of the specified substance in 100 parts of the final product. At 2 H C, it is diluted to one: ten-thousand; at 3 H C, it is one to a million, and so on. At 30 H C, the dilution can be represented by a fraction of 1/1+60 zeros. However, you cannot dilute an active agent infinitely without reaching a point where the quantity of agent in each bottle that you produce. The laws of chemistry set the limit of dilution at which some bottles will end up without one active molecule, and Avogadro, an Italian chemist who was a contemporary of Hahnemann, had already established the total number of molecules contained in a given quantity of a corps.[4] This number sets the absolute limit of a product's effectiveness at 12 H C.[5]

In a stunning experiment publicized in an article in *Science et Vie*,[6] Pierre Rossion revealed the total lack of both activity and toxicity of homeopathic products. Under a monitor's supervision, he ingested ten tubes (that is, 800 tablets) of *Arsenicum album* (the arsenic used by poisoners) covering the entire range of dilutions common in this market (from 4 H C to 30 H C); and he did so without experiencing any toxic effect, nor indeed any noticeable effect at all. And just a few weeks earlier, two children playing at a major homeopathic laboratory had swallowed the contents of several tubes of homeopathic pills that had been "forgotten" in the wastebaskets; in that case, too, there was no discernible effect on their health.

Faced with such challenges to its credibility, homeopathy is continually coming up with arguments to prove if not its good faith, then at least its effectiveness. For example, exploiting the ambiguity inherent in the law of similarity, homeopaths try to lend credibility to the hypothesis that homeopathic solutions act the same way as vaccines, by creating an immunity. (Vaccination is the administration of a weakened form of a substance which, at normal strength, would cause a certain disease; in the weakened state, it protects the subject from the very disease that it ordinarily produces, by stimulating the organism's natural defenses.) But a simple examination of the facts proves that this is a false comparison. Vaccination is practiced on subjects that are *free* of any sign of the disease in order to stimulate *preemptively* the production of antibodies — antibodies which, in the event the subject later comes into contact with the disease, will protect him. This is contrary to the law of similarity, which recommends prescribing "attenuated" substances to individuals who are already suffering from the symptoms of the stated disease.

Another way that certain homeopaths attempt to "legitimize" their work is by comparing the use of the homeopathic drugs with mithridatization* or de-sensitization, through the administration of infinitesimal doses of active substances. However, in the case of mithridatization, the toxic products are administered in gradually increased doses up until the level at which the toxicity should make the subject ill. Similarly, with de-sensitizing, increasing amounts of an allergen are administered in order to stimulate the production of antibodies, preventively. But in de-sensitization, again, the allergen is never given in moment of acute crisis, as is the case for homeopathic dilutions. The somewhat occult aspect of mithridatization may be fascinating, but its effectiveness is far from being proven.

Those homeopaths who readily admit that their scientific reasoning may lack rigor, that their logic may be weak, still persevere in trying to turn aside the challenges that are raised. James Tyler Kent, a contemporary British homeopath and one of the principal references of modern homeopathy, maintains that Koch's bacillus is not the cause of tuberculosis but its consequence.

---

*Mithridates, a king of Pontus, was said to have developed an immunity to poisons by self-administering them in gradually increased doses.

The bacteria are the result of the disease . . . these microscopic elements are not the cause, they come later. They are the result, they are present whenever the disease occurs, and using the microscope we have discovered that every pathology has its corresponding bacterium; but the cause is far more subtle and cannot be shown by a microscope.[7]

Water's Memory

Although it sank into the most absolute absurdity, after having caused a stir initially, the episode of "water memory" must be considered for it illustrates very well what the conjunction of science and illusion can create.

On June 30, 1988, an article was published in the prestigious scientific review *Nature* under the signature of Jacques Benveniste and collaborators, and entitled: "Human Basophile Triggered by Dilute Antiserum against IGE".[7] The title is revolutionary, in itself; and the contents are even more so.

The article seems to show that Benveniste and his colleagues achieved the "degranulation" of basophiles (human white blood cells) by subjecting them to various dilutions of the antibody Anti-IgE[8] (ranging from 10-2 to 10-120) — i.e. dilutions corresponding to the high dilutions used in homeopathy, those in which there is no longer any chemically identifiable trace of the product. A highly diluted allergen agent, placed in the presence of white blood cells, was presented as the cause of an allergic reaction that was evidenced by the degranulation test on the basophiles, thus proving the cogency of homeopathic principles.

This information was big news: if it were proven, it would constitute the obvious proof of the *in vitro* effectiveness of homeopathic dilutions; and the proof was being delivered by a big shot in biology — or someone presented as such — a researcher at INSERM.[9] Better yet: this experiment illustrates the real effectiveness of homeopathic products outside of the psychological effect that is often thrown in homeopaths' faces; it smashes all claims that it is only the placebo effect that can explain homeopathy's claims of success.

The truth is considerably less brilliant. While Dr. Benveniste claimed to all and sundry that he was not defending any pro-homeopath position, it was soon proven that he and some of his collaborators were under contract with the homeopathic laboratories of Boiron, which had commissioned the experiment.

The tests used to demonstrate the basophile degranulation are marketed by a company in which Dr. Benveniste is a shareholder — and he refused to repeat the experiments using similar tests produced by other companies, with which the experiments "did not work".

The term "degranulation" that was advanced to prove the effectiveness of the dilutions turned out to have been wrongly employed; "achromasy" would have been more appropriate. (While degranulation would have been real proof that the basophiles had produced histamines, that is, proof of the effectiveness of the dilutions used, achromasy only reflects a chemical activity unrelated to the release of histamines, and therefore of no relevance as proof.)

Attempts to repeat the experiment under controlled conditions by third parties never managed to reproduce the alleged facts, and "leaving their scientific baggage on this side of the mirror, Benveniste and his partisans have, like Alice in Wonderland, passed through the famous mirror to enter the land of rushing rabbits and mad hatters".[10]

Convicted of fraud, or at least of using unreliable experimental methods, Benveniste did not quit: nine years later, he went as far as to affirm that the memory of a molecule without a molecule is transmitted not only by water (water memory) but also through space, via by computers, which according to him may lead to the development of a therapy and a vaccination that can be used via Internet.[11] Buttressed by a staff of professionals from various fields (economists, engineers, doctors, mathematicians), Benveniste is still trying to explain away the deficiencies of his 1988 "proof".

In his micro-macrocosmic theory, he draws an analogy between galactic black holes and "white holes in water", which he claims would explain the memory of water (and, why not, the holes in one's memory?). Benveniste and Co.'s new theory was discussed in a veritable treatise published under the appealing title, "Theory of High Dilutions and Experimental Aspects".

But Professor Claude Hennion, a researcher at the Advanced School of Physics, says "This is a book intended to mislead its reader, and to a scientist it is completely incomprehensible. Either it is a hoax, or the four researchers are completely insane; but if they think they are being serious then there is something dramatically wrong". Professor Georges Charpak, 1992 Nobel laureate in physics, is ironical: "If all this is true, it will be the greatest discovery in nine years!" Indeed, Benveniste's recent "experiments" are even more astonishing and miraculous than the ones he carried out nine years before, and the underlying theory is based on magic.

According to Benveniste, in the course of dilutions and succussions, the molecule of the active agent gradually, then completely, disappears (this much we knew, without any possible doubt) — but it leaves in its place an empty envelope — a "white hole" that represents, to some extent, its mark. (This seems to be a surprising analogy to the belief in the "vital" mark left by the deceased, which supposedly shows up as photographic evidence of the subsistence of an etheric form on the spot where the death occurred. This also touches on the old illusion that, after death, the eye preserves the imprint of the last thing seen.)

These white holes are, in fact, supposed to be super-luminous points emitting an electromagnetic wave that can reveal hyper-protons (an electromagnetic entity that is new, even to Dr. Charpak). The human body supposedly manufactures, in the blood plasma, in accordance with the rate of the heart beat, white holes that generate remanent (or persistent) electromagnetic waves that cause diseases. . . !

Reaching a new level in para-phreno-magical delusion, Benveniste is not shy to propose techniques for transmitting the "remanent" information from the homeopathic succussions. He asserts that it should be possible to record the electromagnetic wave emitted by a homeopathic dilution onto a computer disk or on any other medium: CD, magnetic tape, etc.. This medium could then be read, making it possible to transfer the recorded signals into pure water, which would then become active and "dynamized" in turn. You can see how wonderful a system this suggests, enabling us to send by mail, email, diskette or Internet the "dynamizing" electromagnetic waves from which new active solutions could be created and thus to "dynamize" the planet and its inhabitants. Experiments carried out by Dr. Charpak's laboratory at the Advanced School of Physics unfortunately were not able to prove the least bit of evidence that could support the cogency of these wild imaginings — which led Professor Jean Jacques, of the College of France, to say, "The memory of water is a vast attempt to make cretins of the general public".

This attempt to make us all cretins, however, seems to be succeeding, if one considers how quickly business is growing at the homeopathic laboratories and how many new homeopathic practitioners hang up their shingles every day. However, simple common sense proves at a glance that the theories on which the memory of water are based are, at the very least, hazy. Since the creation of planet Earth, water has been constantly recycled. What, then, of the therapeutic effect of the urine of dinosaurs or river rats, which must have become incredibly effective in the course of successive dilutions? But that is no problem for Benveniste. Hasn't he even said that the procedure of high dilutions was like having someone waggle a car key in the water of a river, then going to the river's mouth and collecting a few drops of water to start the same car?[12]

Experimental Precedents

Homeopaths have always refused to conduct double blind chemi-cal experiments — that is, experiments carried out in parallel on two groups of patients, one of which receives a placebo while the other re-ceives the drug that is being tested — with the patients and the re-searchers both being in the dark as to which group was which. This type of method makes it possible to eliminate the placebo effect, which compromises any open medical experimentation.

In 1986, *The Lancet* published the results of a double blind experi-ment on the use of pollens at 30 H C in treating hay fever, and the re-sults show a significant reduction in the strength of the symptoms in the homeopathic group, as compared to the placebo group. However, a closer reading of the methodology shows that the first group of patients also took antihistamines during the experiment, unmonitored by the experimenters.[13]

That same year, a new series of experiments was carried out with the intention of establishing the effectiveness of homeopathy, by con-trasting it with a placebo. *Opium* 15 H C and *Raphanus* 5 H C were tested for their ability to aid in re-establishing the transit of gases and matter in the aftermath of abdominal surgical operations. The conclusions of the experiments, which were conducted according to rigorous meth-odological procedures, once again discredited homeopathy and proved instead that it is "effective" on unverifiable clinical signs and ineffective on real clinical signs. No significant difference appeared between a group of patients who received nothing at all, a second that received a placebo, another that was given *Opium* 15 H C and finally the one that received both *Opium* 15 H C and *Raphanus* 5 H C.

Homeopathy has survived other such setbacks in the course of its history — for example during a large scale test that was carried out in Germany in the late 1930's. On August 8, 1937, in Berlin, opening the

International Congress of the Society of Homeopathy in the name of the Führer, Rudolf Hess gave an address quivering with emotion in which he issued an appeal in favor of homeopathy.

> The new Germany considers that it is politically necessary to look into every phenomenon, whatever it may be. However, certain doctors have not hesitated to attack and reject not only new therapies, but others whose origins belong to an already distant past (as is the case today for homeopathy), without even taking the trouble to subject these therapies to serious examination.
>
> That is why I have taken under my protection the XIIth International Congress of Homeopathy in Berlin, in order to express the National-Socialist State's interest in every therapeutic method that is useful for the health of the people.

Following this declaration, homeopathy would make great strides, marching forward in time with the lyric fantasies of the Reich. At the same time, tests were ordered, which were carried out under the direction of Dr. Fritz Donner, a renowned homeopath, and under the supervision of a pharmacologist and an internist.

However, the results were not published; on the contrary, they were completely hidden from the entire international medical community, for many long years. A translation of the report written by Donner in 1966 finally appeared in a French journal in 1969 (the report was never published by the German press). Moreover, the book by Henri Broch,[14] who reported these facts, quotes two letters from F. Donner: one addressed to E. Unseld, President of the Central German Association of Homeopathic Doctors, and the other to H. Schoeler, editor of the homeopathic journal *Allgemeine homöopathische Zeitung*. These long and closely argued letters show, among other things, that:

- the results were *all* negative;
- Dr. Donner was pressured to cover up these results;
- certain *pathogeneses*[15] are purely products of the imagination;
- one can expect to find approximately 1000 symptoms if one gives 30 testers, for one month, only. . . the placebo;
- the final result of a "productive set of experiments" was "in fact, to throw more or less everything into the trash basket".[16]

Dr. Donner adds:

> The real situation of homeopathy cannot be communicated to the homeopaths and cannot be published in homeopathic newspapers. In the best homeopathic tradition, everyone can utter the greatest nonsense in the world and it will be printed; on the other hand, a paper on the solid bases of an important drug against diphtheria will never be published, and any researcher working on its sources will be threatened with immediate dismissal!

Fritz Donner, a homeopath whose critical mind deserves recognition, gave an assessment of this verification of homeopathic methods that requires no further comment: "Complete Failure". And yet, he confesses honestly: "I avoided to the maximum extent mentioning in my report anything that would have proven fatal to homeopathy."

Homeopaths argue that it is impossible to subject their art to traditional experimental procedures because of the individualization of the treatment; this is more a defense strategy than a scientific reality. If all testing procedures suggested are refused by the homeopaths, this refusal is the proof that the treatments are indeed not effective and that the producing laboratories are privately convinced, as are their zealous practitioners, that it would be dangerous to submit to a really independent series of tests.

Oscillococcinum, the Miracle Drug

Personalized treatment is the decisive argument advanced by all homeopaths who deny the value of double blind testing, homeopathy against placebo; they say that this type of test cannot apply to homeopathic treatment because it is adapted to the individual patient, and is not based on pathology alone but also on the "temperament" and the "biotype" of the patient.

However, these same homeopaths, convinced as they are of the need to tailor the treatment to the individual, are strangely quiet when it comes to discussing the value of homeopathic treatments that are broadly prescribed, such as *Arnica*, for various and sundry afflictions, and especially *Oscillococcinum*, the miracle anti-influenza drug that enjoys constant publicity in all the media as soon as the weather turns nippy and people start to come down with colds and flus of all kinds.

In Quebec they call it the "flu-buster". *Oscillococcinum* is one of the ten top-selling drugs in France and it is prescribed for both the flu and the cold, abandoning all the principles of individualized treatment. *Oscillococcinum*, so felicitously named, seems to be a weakened form of some unspecified bacillus of the "coccus" family — pneumococcus, enterococcus, streptococcus and so on. But it isn't! Our *oscillococcus* is the homeopathic dilution of an extract of duck liver and heart. It should be noted that this "original" product takes advantage of a special ruling in the public health code. It is the only product to have officially benefited from a specific measure — allowing it to be manufactured according to the Korsakovian principle of dilution,[17] which was prohibited in France until 1992.

This "drug" has a unique history. In 1919, during a worldwide flu epidemic, a French doctor named Joseph Roy observed an "oscillating" variation in his patients' conditions and an "oscillating" amount of a certain microbe, which he decided to call the oscillococcus. He went on to observe the same thing in a certain number of viral diseases — herpes, chicken pox, shingles — and for good measure, he also detected it in the blood of cancer patients. Fortified by these observations, he decided to test a vaccinotherapy, based on an extract of *oscillococcinum*, on cancer patients. The results were not entirely encouraging; the patients, after suffering a brief aggravation of their condition, died. Not wishing to pick up the *oscillococcinum* from his patients, Dr. Roy went looking for it among various types of animals and ended up discovering it in the liver of the Long Island duckling.

Oscillococcinum was born, and its bright future was assured. Decried by conscientious homeopaths who doubt that its benefits can be universal, it is nonetheless popular among consumers, and today it is promoted by a logistics that is better established than that of other, more effective, products. Will *Oscillococcinum* stand up to the test of time, and will duck liver defeat the flu that originated with Hong Kong chickens? Only time will tell. . .

An Enlightening Editorial

As a prelude to an article on homeopathy in the journal *Research*, the editorial entitled *The Lobby is in Their Heads*[18] summarizes perfectly the problems that this patamedicine creates.

> Once we admit that homeopathic treatment is not based on any active principle, it is easy to understand how it works. Most of the illnesses from which we suffer or believe we suffer are cured spontaneously. Homeopathic treatments, which do not present any risk of side effects, of course, are prescribed during a consultation where the patient is given a better listening (on average) than in the context of a traditional medical consultation, much less a hospital visit. Along with other remedies that go with "alternative medicine", it is thus a more than honorable substitute for medication based on the so-called scientific medicine — at least as long as there is nothing seriously wrong.

These are good times for homeopathy. The art is nearly 200 years old. Its current, undeniable popularity in Europe and North America ties in with the ecologist movement, in the broad sense, and the industrialists know how to exploit that. As emphasized in a pamphlet published by the French homeopathic industry, "Homeopathy fits in beautifully with current trends such as ecological concerns and respect for the body and its biological rhythms". In the United States, homeopathic drugs are generally found in New Age boutiques. The industry is flourishing and it has a strong lobby. In the aforementioned pamphlet, experts in the French laboratories flatter themselves with having played an important role in inventing and publicizing the "new American homeopathic pharmacopoeia". The industry financed the personnel and the work of Jacques Benveniste's team at INSERM, until the man's behavior began to be too annoying. It financed a quantity of clinical trials that were of particularly dubious quality. Through clever lobbying, the industry had a hand in getting the European States to harmonize the conditions under which homeopathic drugs can be sold [so that the same rules and restrictions, or lack thereof, must apply in all the countries of the European Union], by exempting homeopathic treatments from proving their effectiveness — while official medicine is still subject to rigorous testing.

In France (which dominates the world homeopathic market), the commission of experts responsible for advising the Health Ministry on the rate of reimbursements to offer for specific medications renders one opinion after another saying that homeopathic products should not be reimbursed. This opinion is regularly ignored by the Minister, under liberal and conservative administrations alike. At the height of the Benveniste scandal, even the French President François Mitterrand lent his support.

In the United States, where the French homeopathic industry has been waging a 20-year campaign of conquest, the Congress constrained the NIH (National Institutes of Health), the institution that rules over biological and medical research, to create an Office of Alternative Medicines (the OAM) in 1992. This organization has been headed by a homeopath, Wayne Jonas, since 1994. There is an ongoing battle between congressmen favorable to alternative medicines and the leadership of the NIH, supported by some Nobel Prize-winners, on whether to transform the OAM into an institution in its own right within the NIH, with the ability to call for research proposals and to distribute grants. Last September, the respected British weekly magazine *The Lancet*, one of the two most prestigious medical scientific periodicals in the world, published a "meta-analysis" synthesizing several clinical studies on the effectiveness of homeopathy; the analysis concluded that this practice could not be compared to a mere placebo. The article, the methodology of which has been highly criticized, was written by the head of the OAM, Wayne Jonas, who was listed as a principal co-signatory. The article ends by thanking the French and German homeopathic industry.

One of the homeopathic industry's chief objectives is to have this discipline recognized in university courses. In the pamphlet mentioned above, the industry claims to have received the support of the Conference of the Deans of Medical Schools, in 1983. The European Parliament voted in favor of a recommendation along these lines in 1992. In December 1997, the [French] Council of the Order of Doctors picked up this claim in turn and, despite various protests, did not retract it.

The industrial lobby is supported by an ideological lobby that includes some of the leading members of society. Members of the royal families, superstars, and successful businessmen are involved. How can we explain this? There is no clear answer. Certainly, it has to do with the eternal appeal of magic and the notion that it can break chains, that it offers an opening into another realm that is less rational, less harsh, more reassuring. But it is also certain that traditional medicine, which has become scientific medicine — fast, cold, obscure, fallible, and therefore dangerous — engenders mistrust and concern, even in the best minds. Homeopathy, based on scientific and commercial imposture but practiced with sincerity, largely owes its success to people's rejection of traditional medicine.

At a time when talk of trimming the high cost of health care makes it possible to cut hospital budgets and to drastically rein in liberal medical practices, it is astonishing how easily our leaders waste the taxpayers' and welfare recipients' money by diverting several tens of millions of dollars[19] from real care to a field so full of charlatans, whose areas of "expertise" have been growing nonstop since the birth of homeopathy.

Gemmo-Therapy

In the 1960's, a Belgian homeopath had the prescience to recognize that plant buds might present an effective therapy. He seems to have derived his "intuition" from two existing notions: embryo-therapy, the utilization of embryonic cells that Niehans was pushing at about the same time, and homeo-phyto-therapy, which held that certain plants — such as mistletoe — have great healing virtues.

Buds were supposed to conceal the power of an organ in the process of maturation and the spark of life in gestation. Consequently, our doctor conceived what he called "gemmo-therapy", a term that was promptly picked up by homeopathic laboratories in Europe, and offered as a weapon against hair loss, infertility, stress and other evils.

At first, gemmo-therapy followed the traditional course of homeopathic drugs, in other words, it was prescribed according to the good old method of gut instinct, soon coupled with the divining rod. The technique was quickly refined — and the cost to the patient was escalated.

Gemmo-therapy very quickly caught the interest of biologists who had the idea of studying the biological modifications effected in a rabbit after gemmotherapeutic preparations were given, especially modifications measured by plasmatic protein flocculation* tests.

Complex scientific calculations, charts and graphs, quantitative reports and computer-driven number-crunching helps them arrive at a diagnosis, treatment and personal assessment of the patient; this assessment is transmitted to the prescribing homeopath, who ceremoniously passes it on to the patient. The only blot to mar this picture is that the flocculation test for plasmatic proteins is considered unreliable, and has been given up by serious testing laboratories. But is it really necessary to apply a reliable system of analysis to a whimsical technique? That is for the individual to decide — either way, the profits will continue to flow.

Gas Biotherapy

Presented as a medicine derived from the basic field of homeopathy, gas biotherapy is a matter of diluting and dynamizing gases, and injecting them into the patient. Created by one Dr. Fix, the method is supposed to treat allergies, where it claims 70% positive results, and rheumatism, where it claims 60% or 70% success, mainly in relation to carpal tunnel syndrome and arthritis of the knee. Its success in treating anxiety-depression syndromes is explained by the fact that the patient is taken in hand and given closer attention and care, plus the placebo effect. Its defenders recommend it for a whole slew of pediatric pathologies: learning deficiencies, personality disorders, attention deficit, as well as in testicular ectopias.

This technique, which is not founded on any theoretical basis at all, which has been subjected to no clinical testing, illustrates a conscious effort to confound charlatanesque practices with the placebo effect — with injectable treatments as one more "plus" over traditional homeopathic practice.

---

*Flocculation is the tendency to bunch together, in clumps or tufts.

Urine Therapy

Among those therapies that fall halfway between practical jokes and reality, urine therapy heads the list, and it has the merit of a long history.

The Ebers papyrus (an Egyptian medical document written on papyrus) mentions, among other supposed prescriptions for curing eye inflammations, a composition incorporating as varied and odorous ingredients as fly and pelican droppings, human urine, and lizard's, children's, gazelle's and even more often crocodile's excrement. The mud of the Nile, swamp muck, mud and a certain type of earth referred to as "BTJ" are also mentioned as remedies in other Egyptian medical papyruses. Egyptian ophthalmologists also mixed excrements (dried and pulverized) with honey — if at all possible, fermented honey. This mixture was used as the basis for baths and ointments against trachoma and chronic inflammations that withstood any other remedy. Urine was also employed for eye baths, while mud and earth were used to make plasters.

In 1948, Benjamin Duggar discovered aureomycin (a fungus, like penicillin, that is effective against some viruses). This discovery gave new life to old therapies. According to Duggar's research, aureomycin, whose antibiotic functions he revealed, could be found in the earth at the edges of cemeteries. Duggar and his team analyzed this earth and found that it contained molds that had the property of destroying pathogenic microbes and bacteria. Continuing his research, Duggar, who held the plant physiology chair at the University of Wisconsin, showed that urine and feces also had antibiotic properties.

This fact is known empirically, and novels for young people often mention cases of the explorer who "disinfects" his wounds with his own urine. But most of all, Duggar's discovery brought into fashion the old Egyptian pharmacopoeia and thus lent full recognition to practices that had been ridiculed just a few years earlier.

Today, urine therapy has convinced some new experts who pre-scribe it either in direct form — a glass of urine the morning on an empty stomach — or in indirect form, in other words after sterilization, dilution and costly manipulation by a "pharmacist", generally an enlightened accomplice of the prescribing doctor. Direct urine therapy is generally practiced by followers of orientalist disciplines.

How much sense is there in a practice that consists of re-introducing the organism's wastes? As for "diluted" urine therapy, it has as much value as homeopathic pills: production cost — next to none; effectiveness — none at all; but the profits are hefty indeed, for those who prescribe as well as those who prepare the treatments.

Defenders of this patamedicine make reference to ancient Egyp-tian or Chinese practices as an argument in support of their work. But reading the old texts, one finds that when Egyptian doctors prescribed excrement and urine to their patients, their pharmaceutical arsenal was based on the idea that the therapy had to inspire disgust in the evil de-mons and malevolent powers that lay at the cause of the disease. The Ebers papyrus outlines 55 remedies using urine or feces, but always in association with other components that seem more likely to have a genuine therapeutic power. For the priest-doctor of ancient Egypt, urine and excrement were invested with magical-religious powers, as genie-chasers, not with the physiological power that is ascribed to them by today's quacks.

Fecal therapy, too, has grown in popularity today. It is often used by homeopaths to treat diseases of the stomach and the digestive tract. We will not dwell too long on this technique, which was copied from homeopathy and consists in using phials prepared from a dilution of a deposit from the patient, to be taken orally. One has to wonder how valid are the sanitary controls and the permits for distributing such products, which are likely to convey bacteria and mortally dangerous viruses like salmonella, enterococci or typhoid bacilli.

The question is, what stand should the public authorities take?

Indeed, if the product prescribed contains an active agent, it should definitely be subject to hygienic controls before it is commercialized. It must not be produced in every salon and dispensary, because it represents a risk to public health. Producing and distributing it should be a crime, and a crackdown must be ignited. If, on the contrary, the product is completely innocuous, then we are talking about a fake practice, a scam; prescribing or producing the treatment must then be punished as fraud.

Thymus-Therapy

A recent distortion of cellulo-therapy, thymus-therapy is distinguished by how the product is produced. Cellulo-therapy consists in injecting the patient, for therapeutic purposes, with fresh cells taken from animals. THX (or its equivalents) is the product most commonly used. Condemned since 1956 by the Academy of Medicine, this technique keeps cropping up in more or less sophisticated forms, thymus-therapy being — to our knowledge — one of the latest. Thymus-therapists inject a mixture of hormones, immunocompetent substances and enzymes extracted from the thymus.

After vegetating during a "research" phase under the leadership of its creator, Dr. Sandberg, the technique got its real start in 1975, when a THX manufacturing plant was opened in the north of Germany. Since that date, THX has been marketed "under the table", and is used by advocates of patamedicine with the complicity of those doctors who are convinced that it works.

The product is a kind of universal panacea. It is supposed to be as good a treatment for baldness as for lympho-sarcoma, prostate trouble and "mongolism", and it is very much marketed as a miracle cure for cancer. Like the cellulo-therapy promoted by Niehans, Sandberg's thymus-therapy is generally offered to the mature population, because of its alleged rejuvenating properties. Transitory complications are frequent — rashes, itching, fevers, swelling — but they are greeted as the body's healthy responses, as signs that the metabolic processes are accelerating, "rejuvenated" by the treatment.

For this reason, thymus-therapy has joined the great family of Faustian therapies — with cellulo-therapy, the Aslan cures, and Niacin as recommended by the Church of Scientology. They all have one major therapeutic point in common: they are targeted to subjects who are disabled, but who have enough money to pay for the sessions recommended by people writing prescriptions, people who are rather more interested in their patients' wallets than in their health.

3.   NEEDLES AND PAINS

All I want is to learn five or six big words of medicine to enhance my
speech and to give me the airs of an intelligent man.
Molière,
The Doctor Despite Himself.

Patients who are keen to be taken care of like acupuncture even more than homeopathy. Indeed, acupuncture meets many of the criteria of fascination that are lacking in official medicine.

First of all, this is a form of therapy that comes from a remote and exotic country, China, and is laden with the wisdom of two millennia. Regarded as a soft medicine, acupuncture is easy to integrate into an esoteric program, such as that of the Tao. At the same time, it is founded on one of the most material practices, that of moxas (a plant substance, burned on the skin to cauterize it), or of needles, thus combining the physical and the psychic. Lastly, the acupuncture session creates a bond between the acupuncturist and the patient, both of whom become part of the same sacred magical rite; the acupuncture session becomes an initiatory experience.

If there is any similarity between acupuncture as it was practiced long ago and the way it is practiced today, then acupuncture, and phyto-therapy, are certainly the oldest "alternative" medicines. The first known written reference to acupuncture is a comment in *The Book of Springs and Autumns*, from the 6th century BC, with hints of earlier evidence traced on a tortoise shell that was engraved 1500 years before the Christian era.

The origins of acupuncture are directly rooted in magic. The Yin era's ideogram representing medicine was an emblem in the shape of an arrow. On that basis, several authors have hypothesized that there might be a relationship between the ideogram for medicine, certain ritual magic, and the invention of acupuncture.[1]

According to Claire Sagnières, the ideogram for medicine was selected because the sorcerers (shamans) used arrows to kill demons.[2] Many ethnological papers describe the ritual intended to drive away demons — to ward off storms, for example — using a volley of arrows. Voodoo rituals, in which a doll is pierced with needles, are based on the same logic. It is easy to make the leap from the field of symbolism to that of reality and to thrust arrows under the skin, in order to drive out the demons that are lodged in painful places.

All the symbolism of fire and lightning underlie this hypothesis. While lightning is represented in Classical Western art by an arrow (lightning bolts in the hand of Zeus, for example), its visible result on earth is fire — divine fire, projected onto the ground. Chinese acupuncture, since its creation, has relied on the use of fire through moxipuncture, or moxibustion. This consists in heating certain points of the body by holding red-hot sticks close to the skin's surface or by using little cones of burning *Artemisia moxa* or other herbs, positioned over the skin. Cupping, which used to be a popular remedy in many countries, follows the same logic (in cupping, blood is drawn to the skin's surface by applying a cup, mouth down, to the area and creating a vacuum inside it); this technique was used at various strategic points of the body. These practices make frequent reference to fire, and it is probably only the fact that needles are easier to use that led to their becoming more common than moxas.

For some 20 centuries, moxibustion, acupuncture and a related practice in which a mallet, known as "the apple blossom", is used to stimulate points of the body, were common in China. These techniques seem to have reached Europe only at the end of the 17th century, when they were introduced by Ten Rhyne, a doctor from the East Indies Company. They were slow in spreading, until they were revealed to the general public by the publication of the *Precis of True Chinese Acupuncture*, by Georges Soulié de Morant, French Consul in China, in about 1930. During the Second World War, these practices were more or less eclipsed; they returned to fashion in the 1960's and really began making waves in the West after that, buoyed along by the waves of interest in Hinduism, Chinese traditions, and the New Age that were so popular in those days.

In China, however, acupuncture has not always been so successful as we sometimes think. In 1882, the Chinese emperor published an edict prohibiting acupuncture, under the pretext that it was an impediment to medical progress. Acupuncture was reintroduced only after Mao Zedong came to power, and its justification then was purely economic: this cheap technique helped make up for the lack of drugs. So today, in China, people may still resort to acupuncture, but its importance is diminishing day by day and it seems to be increasingly an export product.

Why Acupuncture?

The principles of acupuncture are entirely based on the notion that an individual's vital energy is conveyed throughout the whole body, via special paths called meridian lines. These meridian lines are supposedly accessible from certain points in the skin: the acupuncture points.

All of Chinese medicine is founded on the Tao. In these doctrines, all the elements that make up the world are characterized by a balance (or an imbalance) between the two generating principles of the universe, the yin and the yang.

Yin, the female principle, is associated with the negative pole, with cold, water, the night, the moon, weakness. Yang, the male principle, represents the positive pole, heat, the sun, daytime, strength, energy. All of creation is the result of a subtle equilibrium between the yin and the yang, whose union is expressed in every being and every object that populates the universe. Energy balance is the balance of the yin and the yang within the same body — although that does not mean that the two poles are equal. Every being and every thing is "colored" by yin or yang. Only the Tao represents the perfect yin/yang equilibrium.

Disease was considered an expression of a disturbance in this internal energy balance — too much (or not enough) yin, or too much (or not enough) yang. Chinese medicine thus set out to restore this balance.

This notion of energy equilibrium goes hand in hand with a theory of the origins of the world that is based on five elements: wood, fire, earth, metal and water. Each element is, in itself, an expression of the yin or the yang. Every expression of nature (including pathologies) is the complex result of the predominance of one or more of these elements, together with the balance or the disturbance of the energy balance. This gives you some idea of how complex the theoretical bases of Chinese medicine were; and the Chinese were familiar with traditional anatomy, as well, although they sometimes re-interpreted and corrected it to "adhere" to the requirements of the Taoist doctrines.

For example, besides the "traditional" organs (liver, heart, spleen, pancreas, lungs, kidneys, stomach, bladder, small intestine, large intestine, gall bladder), man and woman were endowed with an additional organ: the great heat source,[3] which does not have any equivalent in traditional Western medicine.[4] Each of these organs has a corresponding meridian line that goes from the surface of the skin to the organ in question, and to the end of the limbs. These are the "subtle channels" that enable the yin/yang energy to circulate and to manage the organism's equilibrium.

The technique of acupuncture would be developed to bring energy (toning up) or remove energy (dispersion) at the level of one acupunctural point. The acupuncturist acts not only in the physiological plane; he works to restore the human being to the "sacred" balance of the Tao.

> The needle as an antenna: In a way, the needle can be compared to an antenna that connects the internal world to its environment. This interpretation goes with the concept that the needle is regarded as a link between man and "heaven" (the environment). This aspect of acupuncture seems to have taken root as soon as the tool was invented: it dates back to the bronze age in China, that is to say around the 17th century before Jesus Christ. And even if, since then, the forms and dimensions have been diversified to correspond with various therapeutic needs, the same inspiration continues to dominate the symbolism. As proof, the traditional range of acupuncture tools comprises nine needles; in Chinese numerologic tradition, the number nine corresponds to "heaven". Thus, the needle remains an intermediary between "heaven" and man, that is, between man and his surroundings.[5]

The points are indexed in various treatises, the principal one being the *Yellow Emperor's Book of Internal Medicine,* but practitioners do not entirely agree on how many points there are: from 160 to as many as 650. It should be noted that the "great Chinese medical tradition" needed a decree from the World Health Organization to set the final number of points at 361.

WHO, to our knowledge, has not yet weighed in with any legislation to standardize the various pulses by which a Chinese doctor can make his energy diagnosis. *The Book of the Yellow Emperor* describes twelve anatomical locations where the pulse can be felt, but there are fifteen types of pulses (described in the *Book of the Pulse,* written in about 300 AD: seven types of superficial pulses (floating, smooth, full, vibrating, relaxed, extended, dicrotic [two-beats]) and eight deep ones (miniscule, immersed, slack, rough, slow, prostrate, damp and weak).

Each radial pulse is divided into twelve parts, corresponding to each meridian line — for which the fifteen types of pulse can be detected. Apparently, Chinese civilization has not been without its own share of quacks and charlatans. If we take the base of twelve pulses, with the twelve meridian lines and the fifteen types of pulse, there are several million possible combinations; and in theory, a different diagnosis should be made for each one!

The practice has had to be simplified as it evolved, and various artifices have been devised to help. Today there are practically diagnostic abacuses which, while they may not work, are nonetheless beautiful works of art. The West, which has always been a sucker for easy solutions, uses acupuncture point detectors based on the principle of the ohmmeter. They detect the acupuncture points the way certain tools help you find a drainpipe inside a wall.

These apparatuses are elegant and come with luminescent diodes giving the most beautiful effect; but they have the frightening habit of lighting up (or failing to) at any place on the body, thus demonstrating that specific points do not exist — or, is it that points do exist that have not been indexed? An elementary analysis of these machines shows that in fact they react to the electrical conductivity and the resistivity of the skin, which vary depending on the thickness of the dermis, perspiration, and several other factors. Thus, "detection" is no more based on reality than a lie detector. But magic is greatly enhanced by such technical supports.

Today, acupuncturists who have been disappointed by the lack of reliable electrical evidence are turning to the detection of variations in the electromagnetic fields at the acupuncture points; here, they are making a theoretical link between acupuncture and dowsing for water.

Does Acupuncture Work?

As a medical student in 1970, I was attracted by various forms of medicine. I enrolled in an acupuncture course (of which the only serious aspect was the prohibitive cost of the texts), for I was filled with enthusiasm by the results that were being published and propagated on television.

I had been particularly impressed by the images of a Caesarean delivery conducted under acupuncture. But my fascination suffered a severe shock the day I had an opportunity to chat with a member of the film team. He told me straight out that the woman who was giving birth had indeed been anaesthetized by acupuncture — but only after having received so many analgesics and tranquillizers that she would have had no trouble sitting down on a fakir's nail-studded board. My personal interest in acupuncture ended that day.

The experiments that have been conducted to prove that acupuncture works have a long way to go before they achieve that goal. In his book on alternative medicine, Jean-Jacques Aulas gave the following assessment of a methodological study carried out by Dutch epidemiologists on acupuncture and headaches — a favorite area of activity for this technique.

> They found that 51 studies had been made. They graded the methodological validity of each study, on basis of 100 points, according to the usual quality standards (number of patients in the study, homogeneity of the groups, how they were selected, the quality of the double-blind technique, etc.). According to these criteria, a study of exceptional scientific rigor should obtain the top mark of 100. In fact, none of these tests scored over 62. And the results of the best tests, those scoring 50 or higher, are completely contradictory. These same epidemiologists had done a similar study a few years earlier of 91 controlled clinical trials of acupuncture in treating pain and asthma and

in weaning people from nicotine dependency. They went over the results with a fine-toothed comb, and their conclusions are incontrovertible. Those tests that seemed to indicate that acupuncture had merit (40 in all) are burdened with more methodological flaws than those that do not show any difference between true acupuncture and a placebo type of acupuncture. These conclusions are very similar to the results obtained by Swiss authors who reviewed a similar group of tests.

Acupuncturists also offer their services to assist in pain management and the treatment of rheumatism. When it comes to controlling pain, it is easy to explain why acupuncture works, through *gate-control* and the production of endorphins.

Gate-control. We have two types of sensory nervous fibers: one type that conveys nerve impulses quickly, another that conveys them more slowly. Strong sensations depend on the slow fibers, while superficial sensations are passed along via the fast fibers. As the nerve impulses move along the fibers, they compete. If a pain is conducted via the slow fibers, it can be short-circuited by fast impulses that saturate the intermediate networks and thus prevent the slow impulse from passing. They act like traffic-barriers: the train comes; the cars stop. This is called *gate-control*.

This is the phenomenon that explains the magical effect of Mommy' kiss on the child's boo-boo. The feeling of a breath or soft kiss (superficial sensitivity) is conveyed by fast fibers and the nerve impulse blocks the feeling of pain (a stronger sensation) by shorting-circuit the relay. Acupuncture acts in the same way: the superficial sensation from the needle puncture saturates the system of transmission and keeps the deeper painful feeling from being perceived — but for that, you don't need either the needle or the specific point.

Endorphins. The second hypothesis explaining how the analgesic effects of acupuncture might work, is based on the human organism's ability to secrete endorphins (natural morphines). This secretion is supposedly touched off when the acupuncture points are stimulated.

I was head of a detoxification center treating drug addicts in 1977, and I met Dr. Wen, of Taiwan, at an international conference organized by the ICAA (International Council of Alcoholism and Addiction). Wen gave a presentation outlining how to get heroine addicts off the drug; he recommended using an electrical current to stimulate Point 54, the so-called "Lung Point", located in the patient's ear. My team scrupulously applied the miraculous procedures that he had presented. We tested 17 patients and had total failure — and the same thing happened in another experiment, testing the ability of electrical stimulation to reduce pain in dentistry. But perhaps that was only due to a poor energy transfer between Taiwan and the south of France!

Head's Zones. In abdominal and thoracic surgery, it has long been known that pain can be mitigated by electrically stimulating certain points in the body; but these points have nothing to do with acupuncture. The cutaneous zones to be stimulated were identified by Dr. Head, an English neurologist. Pain from operations on the esophagus can be eased by stimulating a Head's zone above the thorax; the zone corresponding to the intestine is near the abdomen, and the bladder's is even with the pubis.

Stimulating the Head's zone has a total or partial analgesic effect on the organ concerned, and that is how it was possible to perform the Caesarean deliveries that were presented as arguments supporting acupuncture's effectiveness.

The correlation between acupuncture and the Head zones is easily explained. About two thirds of the "traditional" acupuncture points are located in these zones.

For that reason, doctors at the University of Shanghai have given up the idea of meridian lines in acupuncture — a notion that persists in the West — and have decided to study more closely how the neuro-physiological elements work in connection with the electro-stimulation of the Head zones.

On November 5, 1985, the French television news opened with a documentary that was heralded as something that would revolutionize medicine. Researchers had found evidence of the existence of the meridian lines associated with acupuncture. Professors Albarède, de Vernejoul and Darras had measured the distribution of a radioactive isotope, Technetium 99, and used it as a tracer. They followed the product from the point of injection, all along the leg, to a location in the foot; this was supposed to prove that the meridian lines were real. The announcement had a particularly profound effect since this "discovery" was presented in a communication to the National Academy of Medicine, and the experts were affiliated with the Department of Biophysics and Nuclear Medicine at Necker Hospital.

Amid the chorus of praise, a few voices were raised to express doubts as to the legitimacy of such proof, with the journal *Science et Vie* in the lead. In April, 1986, an article was published under the signature of Dr. Jean Michel Bader, showing the results of an experiment he had carried out in accordance with the protocol described by Drs. Darras, Albarède and of Vernejoul.

The results were conclusive. When a radioactive product was injected at any point in the human body, it spread throughout the body via the blood vessels; and this was true regardless whether the injection was given at an acupuncture point or elsewhere. The "discoverers" had reported that the product, when injected in places that are not acupuncture points, did not spread; this can be explained by the fact that the experimenters had, in all probability, stopped the experiment at the first glitch[6] or had set the oscilloscope to eliminate any zones of low radioactivity, "bothersome" signs of the product's dispersion. According to Henri Broch,[7] the mapping of meridian lines by radioactive tracer is not a real proof but rather real baloney.

Many experiments have been conducted in an effort to prove the clinical value of acupuncture. Some have compared real acupuncture with placebo acupuncture (that is, applied to areas that are not recognized acupuncture points). Others have focused on electro-acupuncture or laser-acupuncture. These experiments provided more insight into the placebo effect.

In one example, non-acupuncture points were "stimulated" with a non-working laser, or one without a needle, in a fake acupuncture session on a zone that is not visible to the patient (his back, for example). The results were as good as those for the "real" technique. Acupuncture without a needle or laser is as effective as real acupuncture — in some cases, even more effective.

The Lancet published an exposé in 1984, devoid of any ambiguity. "Many tests have shown that the claims made in favor of acupuncture have no scientific validity." It repeated the 150-year-old conclusions of the *Edinburgh Medical and Surgical Journal*:

> Consequently, an open mind, a scientific mind (especially considering the diseases for which the greatest successes have been obtained by acupuncture), will be naturally persuaded to attribute the healings so obtained to the influence of the imagination, and will conclude that acupuncture must be banned from the medical practice.

4. Muscles and Bones

> *Drum: After I eat, sometimes I feel a kind of tickling here. It tickles, or rather it prickles.*
>
> *Knock: Wait a minute! Let's not confuse the issue. Does it tickle, or does it prickle?*
>
> *Drum: It prickles. But it also tickles me a little bit…*
>
> *Knock: Does it prickle you more, after you eat calf's brains vinaigrette?*
>
> *Drum: I never eat that. But it seems to me that if I did, then it would prickle me even more.*
>
> Jules Romains,
>
> Knock, or The Triumph of Medicine.

Osteopathy and Chiropractics

Vertebral and articular manipulation must be the oldest physical form of medical care and it probably has come to us, over the centuries, the least changed since its origins several millenniums past. Traditionally the responsibility of bonesetters, it was part of ordinary people's life as well as that of the kings.

The history of medicine — unless the tale is apocryphal — tells us that the Greek physician Galen (129 – c. 199 AD) treated the geographer Pausanias after his chariot had been overturned on the road to Asia Minor. Diagnosing what we would call today a cervical-brachialite with paralysis of the last two fingers, Galen noticed that one of the neck vertebra was displaced; he re-set it and restored to Pausanias the physiological integrity of his cervical joints and the use of his fingers.

Thus, "bone-setting" was added to the bag of tricks used by those with the "gift" of healing throughout the centuries. With their bare hands, these practitioners can perform their miracles on the farmer as well as his wife, a horse or a cow. Rare is the "pure" practice of vertebral manipulation. The bonesetter generally accompanies the mechanical act of re-setting the joint with propitiatory acts, hypnotic gestures or chanting.

Manipulation of the joints and vertebrae, strictly speaking, has made great strides in the United States since 1830. Engineer, doctor, believer and practitioner, Andrew Taylor Still had suffered crippling migraines since childhood. After being relieved by the local bonesetters, especially one Robert Joy, he was convinced of the effectiveness of the manipulation that had been practiced on his person. In parallel, he was disillusioned with the medicine of his era, which had been unable to save two of his children (who died in a meningitis epidemic). With his deep-seated religious beliefs, he spent several years preaching while seeking more effective techniques to mitigate the shortcomings of contemporary medicine. In 1874, he was touched by divine grace. While he was studying a skeleton, an idea came to him: that the essential condition for an organ to function correctly is that its mechanical relations should be in equilibrium with the structures surrounding it and that the various organs and apparatuses of the human body must be in harmony.

Osteopathy emphasizes treatment of the whole person. For an organ or an apparatus to function correctly, it must be under no constraint, of any kind. Andrew Still then stated the basic axiom of osteopathy: "structure governs function".

He also wrote the secondary laws that hold that equilibrium is related entirely to innervation, vascularization and the mechanical equilibrium of the organs. These laws are the principle foundation of osteopathy. "Any pathology stems from an imbalance in the nerves or blood vessels, and this imbalance is, itself, the consequence of a mechanical imbalance" — that is, when something gets out of alignment with the joints or vertebrae. The osteopath's job is thus to identify the imbalance and restore the organ to its initial state of balance. With his hands, he looks for the signs of imbalance and cures it through local manipulation.

Still then plunged into a thorough study of anatomy, osteology and the physiology of human joints. After some successful tests on his close friends and family, he set out on a real adventure by codifying the techniques of what he would come to call osteopathy. In 1892, the American School of Osteopathy was created. Osteopathy took off, fueled by the charisma of its founder and the simplicity of the technique (not to mention its low cost). Osteopathy was quickly recognized throughout the United States and osteopaths acquired the same rights in the U.S. as allopathic doctors.

At the same time, David Daniel Palmer (1845-1913) was founding the chiropractic school of Davenport, Iowa. But he was quickly supplanted by his own son, Bartlett Josua (whose wife made the first glass-plate radiographs of the spinal column). D. D. Palmer would be rehabilitated by his grandson, who, understanding how to do business "American-style", developed chiropractics as a mixture of osteopathy, certain rules of hygiene, a bit of philosophy and a strong dose of religious esotericism.

In 1918, one of Still's students, J. M. Littlejohn, founded the British School of Osteopathy, which then made inroads in continental Europe. The French Society of Osteopathy was created by Lavezzan, Piedallu and Waghemacker. Little by little, osteopathy has gained full recognition (and in Europe, it is expanding its reach); several-year training courses are geared to doctors specializing in rheumatology and rehabilitation. Osteopathy has become a medical practice on its own, aiming to restore patients' full functioning, both physiological and psychological, by restoring harmony to their anatomical structures through a series of precise adjustments.

All this would be fine, if osteopathy had not undergone a further evolution that has nothing to do with modern science: it has been kidnapped by charlatans.

Mechanical Errors

Every year, dozens of patients experience massive neurological complications up to and including complete paralysis, as a result of their visits to pseudo-osteopaths and pseudo-chiropractors.

> Vertebral manipulation is a therapeutic treatment that consists of a short jerk, applied to one vertebral segment that has been identified beforehand and placed under tension. This maneuver often involves a snapping or a cracking sound. This noise is related to the phenomenon of bullization in the articular vacuum. No cracking is necessary for the manipulation to be effective, but it is the evidence that something has occurred in the joint as a result of the treatment, and it very often gives both patient and operator a feeling of plenitude and the accomplishment of a beneficial action.[1]

This feeling of plenitude and complete confidence places patients in a state of total dependence and leads them to accept manipulations that sometimes have dramatic consequences. Beside the benign incidents that Guy Piganiol calls the "vegetative storm"[2], that is, an increase in the pain, nausea, dizziness and aches that often accompany a vertebral manipulation, more serious consequences can appear.

> Manipulation can always create a lesion and the same symptoms that it is supposed to cure (cervicalgia or dorsalgia). Manipulation can decompensate a fragile vertebral state and too-frequent manipulation is dangerous since it can end up transforming acute crises into chronic pain. Manipulation can aggravate a pre-existing lesion and can bring complications to the affliction it is supposed to treat. Rheumatologists often find that it has transformed a case of lumbago into a sciatic nerve problem, or simple sciatica into a paralyzing sciatica, or a neck problem into a pain that affects the arm(s) as well as the neck.

> The most frightening complications are neurological in nature. . . .

They occur during cervical manipulation, especially when the upper cervical vertebrae are involved. The complications can take a benign form (a momentary dizzy spell) but they can be more serious, even dramatic or deadly. They generally improve over time, but they can leave significant and grave after-effects.[3]

Faced with the possibility of such complications, it is obvious that the patient must use his brain and avoid like the plague any osteopaths and chiropractors who are not full-fledged medical doctors. These practitioners go so far in their hypocrisy that they claim to have an official status because they are covered by insurance companies for the practice of their "profession". But simple common sense should convince patients that insurance is not synonymous with competence, and that declaring oneself to be in active practice is not a guarantee of technical expertise.

Osteopathy, Chiropractics and Body Cosmogony

The second level of osteopathy and chiropractics is sketched out in Still's writings: the human body is part of a cosmic destiny, and articular manipulation is mixed up with magic tricks and magnetic transference. Bodily contact though manipulation encourages this transferential aspect of the relationship between one person and another. The touch carries a magical connotation, and often the osteopaths' diagnostic maneuvers begin to resemble a caress or a magical cure-all. The kind of talk one hears at symposiums on natural medicine is revealing on this score.

It is often hard to tell the difference between osteopaths and chiropractors, who are more common in Great Britain and America. The latter are interested exclusively in the spinal column and the trouble that can result from the misalignment of a vertebral joint. The chiropractor's work is usually quick and brutal; this is a kind of manipulation that is supposed to "put the vertebrae back in place". This manipulation is usually accompanied by a cracking sound, which sometimes can be the disastrous sign of major complications related to torn ligaments.

As for the etiopaths, they are not very different, in our eyes, from their cousins the osteopaths — although they, themselves, claim to be different. At most one can note a few differences when it comes to cranial manipulation.

Cranial Osteopathy

Cranial osteopathy has had a resurgence of popularity, although it belongs squarely in the realm of the esoteric. Known by many names (craniosacral therapy, cranial balancing, craniopathy, craniosacral balancing), it is a method that purports to remove impediments to a patient's "energy," by manually aligning the skull bones.

Osteopaths offer theories suggesting that the brain is a biphasic liquid system comprising spinal-cranial liquid and interstitial liquid contained in the dural membranes that line the bones of the head (cranium), go down the spinal column, and come together again in the sacrum. These liquids are in constant flux, as the bones of the head purportedly move minutely in a cycle of expansion and contraction at a rate of some 6 and 12 cycles per minute! The parietal bone supposedly moves from 10 to 25 microns laterally. They say that the cranial bones do not grow together, that synosteosis does not occur. They also talk about a "cranial rhythm", a kind of "primary respiration" in which the parietal bones move by as much as one millimeter; practitioners highly trained in palpitation skills are supposed to be able to detect this motion, especially with their thumbs. Anything that might limit this physiological mobility causes a set of symptoms that until now would have been considered as idiopathic; thus the "interest" in cranial manipulation.

Many studies have been carried out on various subjects; and it becomes clear that this theory of primary respiration has no scientific basis. Moreover, it is in complete contradiction with physics, anatomy, physiology, biomechanics, and even clinical evidence. Under these conditions, we cannot imagine any serious therapeutic applications that would derive from it.[4]

Fascia-Therapy

Fascia-therapy is the latest offshoot of this discipline; it targets the muscular fascias, i.e. the conjunctive membrane that envelopes muscles and organs. This therapy is intended to restore proper blood irrigation of the muscles by relaxing the fascias; deep massage is the means by which this is to be accomplished.

Here again, the border between technical validity and patamedicine is negligible. While one might accept the physiological arguments of the fascia-therapists without too many qualifiers, it is harder to accept the interpretations that they make.

> The goal of the treatment is to rehabilitate forgotten feelings and to draw out the rhythms that have been choked off. The therapist makes a precise reading of rhythms that have been slowed down or blocked. Even in the most inert zones of your body, he will restore mobility and clear the way toward the path of life, which seeks only to be expressed . . .

> The reserves thus extracted from your body will always be expressed softly and warmly. The power of expression of your interior, that is silently begging to be set free, will be expressed, always with a very gentle joy.[5]

Pulsology

Pulsology is an auxiliary to the work of the fascia-therapists; it accords the key role to blood circulation and modifications to it. Here, some physiological elements are mixed up with talk of "energy", in an approach that to some extent recalls Chinese energy medicine.

> Blood transports life, and the elements of the body's "natural pharmacy". The tensions of the fasciae can inhibit proper blood circulation . . .

> The therapist locates the zones of blood deceleration and frees up the circulation, in large blood vessels as well as in the capillaries. To do so, he removes the barriers that oppose the integrity of this river of life, be they physical or energy-based.[6]

If you study carefully the whole gamut of manual "therapies" on the market, you find that it is often a thin line that separates the objective elements grounded in anatomy and physiology from those that are more closely related to a sense of "magic" concerning man in his environment.

Kinesiology

Kinesiology is an example of a distortion of techniques that are based on body control. Under a pompous name derived from an amalgam of physical therapy (kinesitherapy) and physiology, kinesiology and its "educational" side, edukinesiology, are a relatively recent perversion of the psychosomatic techniques suggested as a therapeutic and educational system in the context of the general realm of personal development.

A Short History of Kinesiology

The history of how the kinesiology movement developed illustrates how randomly things have been pieced together for the last thirty years in the health field. The authors start with their intuition, more or less built around a physiological basis or some functional data, and over the course of time they add elements borrowed from other doctrines while trying to make a conglomerate that will be acceptable one way or another to future patients.

In the 1960's, taking chiropractic data on organ-muscular balances as a starting point, Dr. George Goodheart expounded on the relations between muscular organs and groups. For good measure, he added a touch of Chinese energy medicine and described the equilibrium between organs, muscles and meridian lines. In the area of *touching*, Dr. John Thie provided the foundations of applied kinesiology, through the *touch for health*. He introduced the idea of interrelationships between the various systems, an equilibrium whereby one system affects the integrity of another (for example, one's vision cannot be perfect if one's hearing is defective). In this way he defined 14 principal muscles and 28 additional muscles, and established a system of how they were connected, founded on the use of neuro-vascular points, neuro-lymphatic points, and on the scanning of the meridian lines.

In turn, Dr. Denisson created educational kinesiology, or edukinesiology, by stretching the concepts of right brain and left brain — which are major weapons in the theoretical arsenal of New Age medicine, even though they have no real anatomical-physiological reality.

It is true that in right-handed individuals, the left hemisphere is dominant and is used mainly for written and spoken language; however, it is also well known that a person with a cranial trauma, in which some of the left hemisphere functioning has been lost, may be rehabilitated to some degree by "reactivating" the identical structures in the uninjured right hemisphere. By contrast, no clinical experiment has proven that the left brain governs reason and the right brain emotions, as so many trendy techniques suggest — any more than there is one brain for conscious and one brain for unconscious or subconscious processing.[7]

Taking up Goodheart's concept of energy flows, from a new angle, the nutritionist Dr. Jimmy Scott developed a theory that old or recent, physical or psychic obstructions of the energy flow influence our relationship to the environment and predetermine certain pathologies. Thus, he posited that allergies exist because of blocked energy, caused when the subject is confronted with a parasitic energy whose vibrations are not in harmony with his primordial energy, or that establishes resonance with the blocked energy zone (!). Whiteside, Callaway and Stokes then came up with the *one brain/one health* concept, and began working on the emotional causes of psychic and physical disorders, which they felt could be corrected by de-energizing these causes in the past and by liberating the system of conditioned beliefs. They invented the concept of *harmonic kinesiology* (*three-in-one* concept), or *integrated brain*.

Dr. Diamond's behavioral kinesiology would integrate the influence of the environment on the individual (agressology), his way of life (ethology and ethnology), and nutrition (diet), together with the effect of positive and negative thoughts on the individual's energy level. Dr. Bruce Dewe and his wife, Joan, developed Integral Health (Professional Kinesiology Practice) in New Zealand, and expanded the use of energy balancing. Dr. Alain Beardall introduced the concept of the digital determinator, and finally Dr. Verity (a good name) created the *blue print* series that was intended to eliminate the negative ego and to find the origin of our fears — the negative ego being responsible for our diseases and pains, our codependencies and the various inherited beliefs and habits that underlie our repetitive behaviors.

Principles of Kinesiology

Kinesiology uses simple and precise muscular tests to examine the body and identify the nature, the location, the intensity, the history, and the origin of energy blockages so that the therapist can adapt a program of exercises to correct them.

Those who defend educational kinesiology say that its goal is to help people draw on both the right and left hemispheres of the brain during certain activities such as speaking, reading, writing, driving, seeing, hearing, and remembering.

> "It is commonly noted that for most of us, our 'biological computers', our brains, are not programmed very well. Using simple muscular tests, we can test a person to find out how he is organized, what are his dominant tendencies, how the communication is organized between brain and eye, brain and ear, brain and hand, etc.. We can better understand where the blockages or hold-ups occur, and how we can remedy them. It is these blockages that usually cause the difficulties we encounter at various stages of education, whatever our age. They also contribute to our constant stress, to difficulties of concentration and of communication, and they can even create muscular tensions that lead to poor posture. One might say that the body carries in itself the means of doing away with these blockages; using the appropriate tests, KINESIOLOGY can interrogate the body, and thus can understand and read the answers that the body itself offers for the problems encountered. We can then help the body to self-correct, through simple exercises. When we give the body the necessary means to clear up these blockages, we very quickly see a clear improvement in everything that relates to the simplest activities such as reading, writing, seeing, hearing, remembering.[8]

One of kinesiology's recent "discoveries" is that memory is not confined solely in the brain but is also, more or less, in every cell of our body and most particularly in the muscles, muscle groups and fascias, according to precise and unconscious psychological diagrams. Thus, kinesiologists believe that by probing the muscles with appropriate tests it would be possible to tap into this memory and the blockages that it generates.

Let's take a look at some excerpts from an advertising brochure put out by a group on edukinesiology.

> The two cerebral hemispheres are connected by a kind of bridge named the "corpus callosum", a complex bundle of nervous fibers that allows communication and coordination between these two parts of the brain. If, for any reason, this connection does not function correctly, or if it is interrupted, the person will present very serious disorders that will handicap his general functioning. Each hemisphere has a quite precise function.
>
> The right brain governs the "reflexes"; it perceives the overall picture in a given situation. It enables us to recognize a melody from the first two notes, or to recognize faces in a crowd. It serves as the pilot for the left part of the body. The left brain is "analytical"; it breaks up information into minimal units and deals with it sequentially. It is the seat of language and logic. It controls the right part of the body, and is much emphasized in our education system, for it is the hemisphere of logic, which our ... culture so cherishes.
>
> Neither hemisphere holds priority over the other but, quite to the contrary, complementary functioning is the rule, and it is precisely the lack of speedy connections between the two that lies at the origin of slow development in learning, expression, communication. When we talk about predominance, in educational kinesiology, it is in the context of looking to find out which of the two hemispheres the person more readily uses, in a given situation, and why he has trouble integrating and using the whole range of possibilities that he has at his disposal.[9]

This brochure starts off with a correct anatomical-physiological presentation on the existence of the cerebral hemispheres, but then passes directly to an aberrant interpretation of the respective roles of the two "brains". Any secondary school student learns that the reflexes are seated in the spinal cord and not the brain. All the subsequent reasoning is thus off-base and is re-interpreted in favor of kinesiologic practice.

How Kinesiology is Performed

The kinesiologist conducts a muscular test that purports to determine where, when and how cerebral inter-hemispheric coordination is present; then he makes an assessment of what he considers to be a cerebral disharmony. He then uses muscular and gymnastic exercises in an effort to rehabilitate the brain through its muscular connections.

This technique has the merit of borrowing from the disciplines of speech therapy, physical therapy, and functional rehabilitation; but it rests on several theoretical inconsistencies, especially in regard to the brain's role. Furthermore, proponents of this technique present it as the cure to whatever ails you. One brochure suggests that it will eliminate problems including:

- physical: back pains, joint problems, migraines, eczema, colitis, impotence, sterility, ear-eye-nose-throat problems, etc.;
- emotional: anxiety, lack of confidence, stammering, dyslexia, etc.;
- mental: fear, doubts, depression, disturbed behavior, etc.;
- energy: fatigue, sleep disorders, immunity deficiencies, etc.;
- nutritional: obesity, anorexia, diabetes, etc.;
- other: tobacco, drug, or alcohol dependency, relationship problems, development problems (memory, concentration, elocution, coordination), learning problems, etc..[10]

The positive results obtained at "brain gym" sessions with young children are due solely to the additional attention given to the "problem children". But questions must be asked when, in the context of a suggested training curriculum, esoteric concepts crop up that traditionally belong to patamedicine: the law of the five elements, the law of seven dimensions, the seven barometric tests, the four stages of evolution and the twelve forms of energy inversion.

It seems that edukinesiology, like so many other groups, uses education as a Trojan horse in order to get people to accept a message that has more to do with the fantasy of its creators than with the well-being of the participants.

5. GO FOR WHAT'S NATURAL

Clysterium donare postea seignare ensuita purgare.
Molière,
The Imaginary Invalid.

Worshipping the "Natural"

Naturopathy got off to a modest enough beginning. Early in the19th century, an illiterate Austrian peasant named Priessnitz rediscovered the virtues of cold water; he created a hydrotherapy center and laid the foundations of a "purification" technique based on water and a lacto-vegetarian diet. A couple hundred miles away (in Czechoslovakia), another pioneer, Schrotk, was following a similar path, using moist heat.

The technique really took off under the magic wand of one Kneipp, a rural priest whose name would go down in history, inscribed on boxes of breakfast cereal. Kneipp founded an establishment in Bavaria where the cold water cure would be supplemented by physical exercise, hot wraps, a frugal vegetarian diet, and treatments with medicinal plants and clay. The cure sometimes took poetic forms; for instance, Kneipp recommended his patients walk barefoot in the morning dew. Kneipp energized his crusade with the claim that he had cured himself of pulmonary tuberculosis.

Tuberculosis also struck another cheerleader of natural medicine, one Dr. Carton. After having healed himself (right, him too), spontaneously, Dr. Carton developed, on the basis of his personal observations, a regimen of care in which natural food, detoxification, physical exercises, hydrotherapy, and baths of air and sun are all intermingled.

This brings us to 1906, when there is as yet no real medicine for tuberculosis, and the usual cure prescribed was to spend time in the mountains and sunshine. Carton's theories did not meet with unmitigated success. Perhaps this is due to the intellectual vagaries of their author, who switched both his political and religious allegiances before falling gradually into oblivion.

Carton's trajectory was part of a social movement having to do with a new interest in the human body, which came into vogue after the First World War. Naturopathy had its first successes in the form of body-building, with two famous "Masters", Hébert and Marcel Rouanet. The first company-paid vacations for workers enabled the average family to rediscover the countryside, the sun and the sea, but the "debauchery" of the working class led the adherents of the Aryan ideal to rediscover the noble values of a perfect body.

Soon enough, it was the hour of glory for biological humanism, pioneered by Marchesseaux. Little by little, worship of nature gave way to worship of race, and the detoxification of the individual body was inconsequential within the context of a polluted social body. While calling for combat "for a new humanity — healthier, more lucid, more charitable, in a better world with no violence", Marchesseaux wrote columns for the periodical *Vérité* [*Truth*], and became the herald of the movement to bring sexual deviance under control through naturopathy. To combat the overpopulation of the planet, he called for a quantitative and qualitative reduction of the population. He proposed using a battery of morpho-physiological criteria and various athletic tests to select the best parents, who would be the only ones with the right to have children (the others were not to be mutilated, however, nor deprived of their rights to love). Of course, such a program would require great wisdom on behalf of both the leaders and the led. "This should not be allowed to degenerate into a cheap racism like we had under Hitler."[1] These remarks strangely evoke Lebensborn, of the Third Reich, despite the writer's claims.

Fortunately, not all the naturopaths and naturo-therapists preach such ideas. Still, the ideological basis, *Mens sana in corpore sano*, sometimes takes on worrisome Platonic tones, such as: "Health cannot be bought. Bodily conduct reflects mental conduct. A health code is above all a moral code. . .".

And, it is relevant to mention that still, today, naturopathy is taught to non-doctors by institutes where the natural aspect is emphasized within a religious context with strong mystical connotations: "Distancing oneself from the natural is distancing oneself from God, social production is a sign of evil, . . ."

Naturo-Therapy

Given the confusion that now reigns between those who go in for "natural medicine" as practiced by non-doctors, and doctors who are eager to restore some "naturalness" to their daily work, a diploma of naturo-therapy has been created at the respected Bobigny School of Medicine, within the university diploma of natural medicine. Naturo-therapy is thus addressed to qualified medical assistants and ancillary medical personnel, as a field for non-doctors.

Naturo-therapy proclaims itself to be the "medicine that looks for the causes of the disease and which, through the natural comprehension of the clinical signs and phenomena, biological and physical, recommends treatments that tend to reinforce the organism's own defenses" — not exactly a remarkable medical revolution, in our opinion. What is interesting in this approach is the desire of the naturo-therapists to dissociate themselves from naturologists of all sorts.

However, it is disquieting to study more closely the naturo-therapy diagnostic and therapeutic approach, an approach that incorporates all the usual patamedicine gibberish. The naturo-therapists' charter, while it is fairly clear, is still troubling:

> A naturo-therapists is a doctor who has distanced himself from hos-
> pital medicine, which is inhuman and sometimes dangerous; he is a
> health teacher, a hygienist, a doctor of the environment and life
> style . . . He tries to restore the energies of life, which are often non-
> existent because they have been masked by pathological causes. He
> is an esthetician: people in good health are good-looking.[2]

Naturopathy

While the doctors of naturo-therapy are hardly beyond all criticism, the non-doctor naturopaths are quite as skilled in the area of the
irrational.

> Every living being is animated by a vital force. This life energy is an
> intelligent force that is always biased toward health, throughout all
> the hazards of existence, and it confers upon us a capacity of self-
> healing.

> One of the most remarkable actions that this self-healing force reveals
> is cicatrization: wounds close up and bones knit together again. . .
> naturally! But the organism has many other "tricks" by which we cure
> ourselves:

> • Fever, which increases the body temperature, enabling the body "to
> kill" viruses and germs;

> • We cough, sneeze, and blow our noses; we ooze; we peel; we get
> pimples. In a word, we e-lim-i-nate! Another natural way of being
> cured. . .

> So disease, in fact, is used. . . to protect life!

> Relieving the symptoms alone (fevers, pain, cough, blemishes, etc..),

without understanding what causes them, is acting against Life and preparing the organism for real organic or degenerative diseases which will destroy it by less overt means.

The naturopath is the ally of your self-healing vital force: he stimulates it, works with it, awakes its power; he helps you to restore, within you, the conditions necessary to health.[3]

Whatever they call themselves, naturopaths or naturo-therapists, the successors of Kneipp and Rickli[4] work in similar ways. Naturopathy and naturo-therapy cures have three stages:

1. Detoxification, intended to cause or encourage the elimination of humoral (fluid) overloads;
2. Revitalization, which is supposed to fill in any morbid and electrolytic deficiencies;
3. Stabilization, the goal of which is to balance the exchanges.

Marchesseaux, the pioneer, taught that orthodox naturopathy is organized according to the three hygienic processes of eating, relaxing and exercise.

The general doctrines of naturopathy follow the general criteria of "societal" intoxication and "natural" detoxification.

Here are the doctrines. We poison ourselves:

- At skin-level, with certain alkaline soaps, beauty creams, and deodorants;
- At the lungs through smoke, tobacco, pollution, emotional tightness, lack of exercise;
- In the liver and intestines, through alcohol, tobacco, drugs, coffee, sugar, drugs, fat, additives;
- In the kidneys, through excessive salt, lack of water, chemical drugs, excessive meat;

- Generally, through toxic metals, lead, mercury, arsenic, cadmium, and aluminum.

The entire therapy aims at natural detoxification. The detox cure consists in adopting a lifestyle that accentuates the normal elimination of toxins accumulated in the organism at the level of the four emunctories which are: the skin, the lungs, the liver and intestines, the kidneys.

You can start your detoxification with a monodiet in which you eat only one kind of food (depending on what disorders you are experiencing) for a certain length of time, or you can fast for a certain period — this is the most effective means of cleaning out the organism. The fasts can be wet (drinking nothing but water) or dry (the patient takes no solid food nor liquid food).

The detox cures last two to three days and can be repeated regularly.

Except for emergency cases, in the event of feverish or nonfeverish disease, we prepare for this cure by gradually eliminating from our food: first, animal products; then stimulants; then fats and crude oils, cooked grains, cooked vegetables and fruits; and finally the mixtures of raw cereals, vegetables and fruits.

After this cure we begin to eat again, and start the cure of revitalization; foods should be added back into the diet progressively (a monodiet is recommended).

Finally, the stabilization cure enables us to find the correct food combinations and to avoid disastrous associations, although the various schools do not agree on which food associations are those are.[5]

Besides the traditional naturopathic line, such as Marchesseaux's school, new practices have appeared such as the Kousmine method, which set out to revolutionize the treatment of serious illnesses and of cancers in particular. This method comprises a strict food regime.

- You may eat cereals;

- Do not combine foods;

- In fact, eat lightly: steamed vegetables, a little meat, dairy products, raw vegetables and fruits;

- Pay particular importance to breakfast, with Budwing cream in particular (which contains light, soft white cheese), sunflower oil, the juice of half a lemon, a banana, a seasonal fruit with pulp, two teaspoonfuls of whole grain (buckwheat, oats, hulled barley, brown rice), a teaspoon of oleaginous seed (flax, sunflower, sesame, almond, walnut);

- A light lunch;

- A very very light dinner.[6]

In spite of the success of Kousmine's works, his regimen has never, so far, saved a single cancer patient, and it represents one of those dead ends into which patients are lured when they are under stress from having the disease diagnosed and under a psychological burden induced by the treatments.

Dental naturo-therapy is an offshoot of naturo-therapy. Here, we can quote an article by Dr. Montain on dental naturo-therapy; it appeared in the *International Review of Unconventional Medicines*, and it presents both the technique and its limitations.

> Respecting the Hippocratic principle, *Primum non nocere*, the naturo-therapist will be careful not to poison the organism of his patient. Any time that this becomes necessary, he will cleanse it, using the natural methodology and applying the principles of the hygiene of life, in an individually-tailored way. Toxic metals such as mercury, copper and silver contained in the fillings will be removed...

> We prefer [to fill teeth using] alloys based on gold and ceramics. Even with these, prudence is required; some alloys contain only very little gold, and the tests that we have conducted with our Geiger counter reveal that many ceramics are radioactive![7]

One might wonder what level of radioactivity was detected in such a case. It is true that dental naturo-therapy aims at restoring the wave and vibrational balances of which pataphysicians are so fond.

In fact, Dr. Montain poses a fundamental problem in patamedicine, that of good faith and of how open to critical judgment an expert can be who is convinced of a technique that he intellectually believes in and wants to believe in, but that is not backed up by any technical and scientific arguments that can make it credible. Admittedly, heretics have often been the ones who stimulated of the development of science — Galileo stating that the earth revolves around the sun, Einstein working out the theory of relativity — but unfortunately for humanity, heresy is more often the bearer of errors than of truth.

Colonics

Hydrotherapy of the colon occupies a prime spot in the array of bizarre treatments offered in naturopathy. Most people have forgotten the enemas recommended by our grandmothers.

> The first goal of colonic hydrotherapy is to deeply cleanse the intestinal mucous membrane. But it is also, and perhaps especially, a diagnostic method that enables us to check the functional state of the large intestine and to make connections between the patient's symptoms and any disturbances in the large intestine's functioning. This method enables us to determine the presence of intestinal gases as well as the size, the concentration and the location of accumulated feces, as well as the density and the color of intestinal mucus, signs that can help us to determine, for a given person, which types of food encourage the accumulations and thus what kind of diet must be followed throughout the cure, and for the entire period of detoxification of the organism.[8]

The technique: colonic hydrotherapy is a process of cleansing the large intestine; it consists in bathing it with fresh, tepid, purified water, without the addition of chemicals or drugs. Successive baths are carried out, with water introduced and eliminated via a double nozzle introduced into the rectum.

Colonic hydrotherapy claims many and varied beneficial effects: weight loss, prevention of colon cancer, treatment of cystitis, ovaritis and dysmenorrhea, improvement of renal function, recovery after general anesthesia, rejuvenation, treatment of paraplegias and quadriplegias, treatment of low fertility, clearing up skin problems, and a wide range of pulmonary, gynecological, vascular, neurological, and psychiatric disorders. . . In short, hydrotherapy is a universal and beneficial practice that Molière and his doctors would have loved. Unfortunately, it seems that the arguments of the colo-therapists have not succeeded in convincing the infamous technocrats of the Health Ministry, for a decree banned the marketing of colonic hydrotherapy devices in France in 1993.

6. STEINER'S HEIRS

Rudolf Steiner was born in 1861 in what was then the Austrian Empire. He very early discovered the works of Goethe and became a passionate admirer; he later named his research center Goethanum. He joined the Theosophic Society in 1908 and quickly became General Secretary of its German section. Steiner gradually moved away from theosophy and began to study Christian esotericism. In 1913, he broke off definitively with the Theosophic Society and created the Anthroposophic Society, a sort of secret society organized around the "mysteries", initiatory ceremonies inspired by esoteric Christianity.

With the advent of Nazism, the anthroposophs and the future National-Socialists partially came together, at first in the form of ideological conferences. But the Steinerians ended up opposing the Nazis, and the latter set fire to the original Goethanum. Such persecutions brought an end to the exchanges between the two groups, which then competed with each other through the esoteric dichotomy of Steiner's white magic against the black magic of the Nazis. From the beginning, the anthroposophs had close ties with the supposed descendants of the Cathares* — bonds which persist to this date. Even today, certain

*a medieval religious sect that emphasized purity

movements claiming to be linked to or inspired by the Cathares practice a Steinerian form of medicine.

When Steiner died in 1925, in Dornach, Switzerland, he left behind 40 books and the text of almost six thousand speeches that constitute the anthroposophic "heart" of the movement. Steiner not only left his disciples an ideological foundation, he created a complete mythology around his person that helps lend to anthroposophy a mystical-religious dimension that compares the Steinerian man to a solar Christ as well as a hard-to-grasp Nietzchean character.

The influence of Steinerian thought is especially discernible in a number of movements that claim to be affiliated with the Anthroposophic Society of Dornach, or that have assimilated into their teachings more or less clear references to Steiner — for example, the Grail Movement and the Order of the Solar Temple.

In fifty years, anthroposophy has become a universal movement with a strong presence in Germany and all across Western Europe (Switzerland, Belgium, France). It has inspired an educational movement through the Steiner and Waldorf schools. It forms the basis for biodynamic agriculture and has created its own medical movement with the Anthroposophic Medical Association and the Association for Curative Pedagogy and Socio-therapy.

Anthroposophic Medicine

Not very well known under its own name, anthroposophy is the inspiration behind a number of philosophical, initiatory and esoteric movements, as well as associations that use methods recommended by Steiner: astrobiology, bio-dynamy, and eurhythmy. The Steiner techniques combine information from astrology, geo-biology, and magnetism, all in the theosophic context that governed its creation. Steinerian philosophy and practice are based on three fundamental principles:

- The universe is a whole, and interdependences within it determine a person's destiny;
- All forms preexist as an etheric force;
- The human being is characterized by a bipolar system.

It is not revolutionary to observe that the universe constitutes a whole, in which the parts are interdependent — but Steiner's applications build out in two directions. The first is an esoterist vision of biological activity that falls under the classical tradition. This is the: "That which is above is like that which is below" of *The Emerald Table*.[1] This vision enables a number of cults or supposedly esoteric movements to recycle anthroposophic ideas. The second is the exoteric vision of interdependence that takes the form of astrological determination, which is a huge success mainly in biological agriculture circles.

Biodynamic agriculture uses neither chemical treatment nor manure — which seems to be praiseworthy enough — and it invokes the influence of the cosmos in controlling the growth of plants, which appears more dubious. Thus, the anthroposophs hold that when the moon enters a constellation of the "water" sign, it encourages activation of the growth of leaves; when it enters a constellation of the "fire" sign, it facilitates fruit-bearing.

One finds similar ideas at the medical level, where physiological phenomena are interpreted in correlation with the astrological personality of the patient. Depending on one's goals, the treatments will have to be administered while the moon is rising or descending, and will or will not work depending on the astral configuration — this theory comes to its apex in asserting the alignment of the stars at the moment of conception determines the baby's gender.

For the anthroposoph, every form of life is preceded by an etheric force that predetermines the appearance of the vital structure, and its mode of growth, as well. Thus the physical details of an individual are defined by the etheric force that induces them. This force is supposed to make the organism grow into specific shapes. For example, the radial structure of a starfish is induced by an etheric force that is different from one that would produce the spiral shape of a snail or the form human being. The etheric force varies according to whether the human is white or black, large or small, thin or large. By discovering and perceiving these subtle forces, we can diagnose a living organism, and by discovering analogies between one etheric force and another we can begin to comprehend both normal and pathological physiological phenomena. Anthroposophic thought is steeped in the influence of theosophy, of which Steiner was a long-time follower.

Lastly, for anthroposophs, any human organism, from the simplest to the most complex, is a bipolar system. It is composed of a "metabolic" pole made up of the abdomen and the limbs and of a "neurosensory" pole that consists of the head, where thought resides. Between these two poles, a buffer zone is made up of the thorax, heart and lungs; it represents the organism's "rhythmic center" — in reference to the heartbeat and respiratory rates.

This bipolarity is reproduced at the macrocosmic (universe) level and at the microcosmic level (the cell). This microcosm/macrocosm resonance explains how planets act on the various human organs. For anthroposophs, Mercury acts on the lungs, Venus on the kidney, Jupiter on the liver, the sun on the heart, etc..

Looking back at the age-old belief in alchemy, we see that alchemical medicine traditionally assigned a metal equivalent for each planet. Anthroposophic medicine picks up this idea of astro-metal-organ partnerships and assigns to each organ a particular metal: gold, silver, iron, copper, mercury. Anthroposophic medical prescriptions relate to these organ-planet-metal correlations, and accord a large role to metal prescriptions.

For anthroposophs, man consists of four elements:

- The physical body is the one that we perceive daily — a kind of packaging, the form in which the apparent life of the organism is housed;

- The etheric body is a twin of the physical body. This is what animates the naturally dead physical body and gives it life;

- The astral body is the engine or psychism of the contents of the heart. The emotions, instincts, desires, passions and impulses are expressions of this astral body;

- The ego, or human spirit, is what gives the organism its particular configuration. It is the ego that emanates the force that impels the human being to stand up on its legs, to think, to speak.

Steiner's theories on life, health, disease and man's role in the universe led to the development of a complete medical model that offers answers to questions of diagnosis, thanks to crystals; of treatment, by active eurhythmy and fermented mistletoe; and of prevention, by biodynamic food.

Some of these elements have been partially taken onboard by certain groups, whether or not they claim any affiliation with Steiner.

Sensitive Crystallizaton

In 1930 one of Steiner's followers, an anthroposoph by the name of Pfeiffer, developed a diagnostic technique that he called sensitive crystallization.

The sensitive crystallization test is conducted by taking an aqueous cuprous chloride solution combined with a substrate of vegetable, animal or synthetic origin mixed with twice-distilled water, and allowing it to evaporate on a circular plate of glass. This produces a characteristic crystalline solution of the substance. Depending on what type of substrate is being tested, the anthroposoph doctor will see characteristic shapes materializing; these can be analyzed according to a systematic description compiled by anthroposophs over the course of the last fifty years.

For anthroposophs, the image thus created can be used to assess the energy level of the substance under study, whether it is a kernel of corn or a chickpea; it also enables them to assess the loss of etheric substance via bronchial secretions or a drop of blood. This handy technique is thus useful in biodynamic agriculture (for measuring the natural energy of a grain, for example), as in medicine, where it helps in making a diagnosis.

Anthroposophic doctors say that a healthy organism, enjoying a satisfactory energy balance, is identified by a crystallization image that presents radiant and harmonious rays. By contrast, an energy imbalance results in more or less marked disturbances of the rays according to the degree of pathology: then one has only to study the disturbance in order to make a diagnosis.

Each organ should produce a typical shape. This means that it should be possible to identify a sick organ by examining the geometrical form produced during crystallization and by comparing it to the reference images.

Pfeiffer was probably influenced by the ideas of Rorschach, and his practice of assessing personalities based on interpretations of the ink-blot test; however, Pfeiffer seems to have forgotten a fundamental element. Rorschach, in his ink-blot tests, interpreted his patients' personalities on the basis of projections made by the patient himself. If any analogy can be drawn between Rorschach's and Pfeiffer's techniques, it is not where the anthroposophs claim. Rather, it seems likely that, in the spots resulting from their sensitive crystallizations, the anthroposophs see only what their own imaginations project there.

Curative Eurhythmy

Anthroposophy as creative performance — eurythmics claims to be a "direct" expression of a rhythm that pervades nature and is supposed to bring in a "harmonizing process" that influences diseased organs, the "astral body" and the "etheric body". According to the principle of the binary structure of the human body centered around its rhythmic center, an imbalance of the organism entails a rhythmic disorganization of the center. The balance that is thrown off by this dysrythmy is restored using techniques intended to re-center the subject on a fundamental rhythm. Curative eurhythmy was proposed as a therapy in the course Steiner gave to doctors in 1921. It is based on elements of language, used as mantras. The subject must utter certain sounds, accentuating specific vowels, consonants or other sounds that match his own inner resonance. Curative eurhythmy is supposed to act on the various parts of the body by setting specific organs in vibration, and it is supposed to gradually reconstitute the organism's rhythmic balance. It is supplemented by artistic activities and a dose of chromotherapy.

The artistic activities are supposed to establish physical forms around the subject, in his interface with the external world, that are intended to recreate balance among the etheric forms. To that end, the patient adds to his program of bodily expression (the essence of eurhythmy) a creative program involving sculpting, painting or building geometrical shapes, with the goal of creating actual waves of that form around the subject. (This idea about waves emanating from a given shape crop up in a number of cult groups — Horus, for example). In the Steiner centers, making shapes is supplemented with the use of colors, in order to establish a color environment that is related to a color/illness relationship as well as to a metal- or astral-based patient/color relationship.

For the three activities — curative eurhythmy, making shapes through artistic creation, and setting up a subject/color resonance — the patient brings harmony to his coenesthesis* and to his audio and visual surroundings that should restore the rhythmic balance that has

---

* Psychological term for an ensemble of sensations, such as sickness or health, that make us aware of our body's condition.

been upset by the disease.

The private Steiner clinics that specialize in "cancer treatment" have thus crafted a regimen of care made up of creative and eurhythmic activities, plus hot baths aromatized with various plant essences (chosen according to what type of tumor is involved and what energy vibration is required), underwater massages and injections of fermented mistletoe. Surgical operations are accepted, but anthroposophic doctors refuse and counsel against radiation treatments, which change the energy balances and disturb the etheric bodies, thereby "damaging the astral body". . . As a complement to the recommended cancer treatments, the patients must consume only vegetarian food produced using "biological culture" or biodynamics, and no flesh-colored food, which causes energy disturbance.

Mistletoe Therapy

The principle cancer therapy recommended by Steiner, and picked up again today by his disciples, is founded on mistletoe, the holy plant of the druids.

According to Steiner, cancer occurs when cellular balances are disrupted and escape control by the etheric forces. To restore these balances, the organism must be given a product that escapes, itself, the rules of universal balance as conceived in the world of Steiner. According to him, mistletoe is a case in point. A mistletoe seed, having been eaten by a bird, is deposited on a tree. If the seed finds favorable ground, it develops and provides a robust plant that flowers in winter. Moreover, its synthesis of chlorophyll does not correspond to the traditional rules of photosynthesis. For Steiner, the characteristics of mistletoe are a brilliant example of the sacred character and the universal therapeutic applicability of this so unorthodox plant. Mistletoe extract — Isorel/Vysorel, Iscador, or Viscum album — consequently represents the supreme therapy offered to fight the aberrant proliferation of cancerous cells.

This kind of reasoning may have passed muster in 1925, when Steiner died, but it is hard to understand how it can find an audience today; yet it is still one of the therapeutic pillars of Steinerian doctors, who are eager to extend its "effectiveness" to AIDS. To them, AIDS represents a collapse of the person's core, which they call the "I". The lack of cohesion and identity of this "I" are considered the principle explanation of the vulnerability of the "people at risk", such as homosexuals and drug addicts, for whom the lack of identity is indeed a problem.[2]

While Steinerian and anthroposophic practices need not be dismissed altogether (the relaxing effect of eurhythmy may have some validity), they are of no real therapeutic interest and can prove to be dangerous, even fatal, when they divert the patient from sensible medical practices — as is the case with the Steiner treatment of cancers.

One has to wonder how people can believe in the Steiner and Waldorf schools, and the anthroposophic doctors, and one should call a crime a crime — as when a patient is deprived of the benefits of modern therapies (like radiation). But Rudolf Steiner's history apparently grants the anthroposophs a kind of moral exemption that forbids doubt or criticism.

7. EVERYTHING IS IN EVERYTHING — AND VICE VERSA

True, without error, certain and most true: that which is above is as that which is below, and that which is below is as that which is above, to perform the miracles of the One Thing.

And as all things were from One, by the meditation of One, so from this One Thing come all things by adaptation.

The Emerald Tablet of Hermes.

While today's patamedicine experts seldom proclaim themselves disciples of the god Thot (more commonly known as Hermes Trismegist), a number of their diagnostic and therapeutic techniques are directly inspired by the principles of Thot, the revealed word, and the basis of Western esotericism, and at the same time the inspirational source of all the esoteric movements that claim a traditional affiliation.

"Son of Zeus and Maia, Hermes is the least Olympian of the Gods".[1] He represents a divinity that is accessible to human beings. He has a magic rod, the caduceus, which enables him to cure people and to break spells. He is god of both thieves and of doctors, a disastrously prescient combination.

The principles of similarity between the microcosm and the macrocosm are attributed to him — principles which, re-considered by patamedicine, led to the discovery, in each organ, of the image and the principles of the bodily Whole.

The systematic study of iridology, auriculo-therapy and foot reflexology open a window on how people develop new patamedicines, using the patients' attraction to the irrational as their starting point.

Mythological, pseudohistoric, magic, and astrological elements combine, and elements derived from real disciplines of medicine — physiology, embryology — are grafted on, but are reinterpreted in the quasi-fantastical context of the technique in question.

Iridology

Iridology (eye analysis, iris diagnosis) is only a diagnostic technique, and that is all it claims to be. From the technical standpoint, it consists of examining the structure and the pigmentations of the colored segment of the eye — the iris. Hippocrates (approximately 460-375 BC) had already declared: "As are the eyes, so is the body." Physiognomists had long noted that people's eyes change expression and that their pupils change size. They thought these changes were related to sensitivity and certain specialists thought they might be signs of disorders of the nerve centers.

Ignaz von Peczely, born on January 26, 1826 in Hungary, is regarded as the father of modern and scientific iridology. While caring for an owl with a broken leg, Peczely noted a particular spot in the owl's eye, and he associated the mark on the iris with the fracture of the leg. He reproduced this experiment with other animals, and developed the theoretical basis of iridology. According to his theory, every organ in the body has a corresponding area in the iris, and the iris is like a map giving warning signs of various physical, mental, and spiritual problems.

His first book, *Discoveries in the field of therapy and naturopathy. Introduction to the study of the diagnosis by the eyes,* was published in 1880. His many disciples quickly propagated the technique throughout the whole world. For Peczely and his followers, the eye is divided into zones that correspond to the various parts of the body. There is an iris somatotopy, or an organic map, where each organ is reflected in one particular location. This mapping takes place in two stages. The first, circular somatotopy, is the study of the six concentric reflective zones located around the pupil. The second, complementary, part makes it possible to locate the various regions that reflect specific systems and organs; it is the study of organic topography.

Iridologists thus believe it is possible to examine the iris and make a genuine dynamic evaluation and determine the level of the patient's energy resources, by studying the structure of the iris stroma (the matrix of the iris), which is supposedly the reflection of one's overall mineral reserve. This matrix can be fine (that is best) or normal, loose, vacuolar or lacunar (such bubbles or gaps are "evidence" of the utmost devitalization).

Next, the relief is studied. It can be normal, irritated, rounded or flattened — a sign of weakness, depression, general fatigue. Next comes the sympathetic nervous system, which accelerates the vegetative functions of the body. The study of the parasympathetic nervous system is based on the dimension of the pupil, its off-centering (if any), a possible flatness that would indicate the reflective mark of the defective organ, or ovalization.

According to iridologists, analyzing the iris enables us to define our physical constitution and our fundamental heredity.

They describe two major constitutions in this way:

1. The fibrillary lymphatic constitution, which includes blue eyes and all the variations. This type of constitution runs the risk of allergies, etc. (asthma, eczema, migraine, coryza, rheumatism, arthralgia. . .);

2. The pigmentary hematogenous constitution, which is conducive to circulatory problems, to obesity and diabetes, to liver and kidney trouble, and nervous spasms of the digestive system.

Like the homeopath, the iridologist studies the morbid diatheses (congenital predispositions to certain diseases). This encompasses a whole range of problems that successively or simultaneously might befall the same subject, problems that differ as to where they strike and what symptoms they produce, but supposedly are identical in nature.

The diathesis implies an overall unity of the disease and its causes, in spite of its various somatic manifestations.

There are four major diatheses:

1. arthritic allergic hypersthenic. The patient is often optimistic, enthusiastic, and passionate, but may evolve toward asthenia;

2. arthritic infectious hyposthenic. The subject is pessimistic, careful, sparing, is more prone to reflection than to action, with infectious tendency;

3. neuro-arthritic dystonic. The patient is prone to nervous hypertension, anxiety, aerophagia, and aerocolics;

4. anergic or asthenic. This is the ideal breeding ground for the major diseases of our civilization: tuberculosis, nervous disorders, multiple sclerosis, Parkinsons, suicide.

Iridology thus should make it possible to establish a complete panorama of the individual's vital potential, his heredity, morbid predispositions, imbalances and deficiencies.[2]

However, a simple examination of iridology theories shows that this is, in fact, a diagnostic technique worthy of Molière's Diafoirus. That does not prevent iridology from claiming to be a natural outgrowth of classical medicine and from claiming that its origins date back to "before 1000 BC"; and that it is "in agreement with genetics and embryology".

> In that remote era, man contemplated the sky, he observed nature and the various relations that exist between beings, things, and events. These observations led him to note that there is a correspondence between the human body, divided into twelve parts, and the twelve signs of the zodiac; thus the laws of the earth and the heavens were interpenetrating, and the man of remote times looked into the eyes to assess the state of someone's health.[3]

Here is the microcosm/macrocosm analogy that is supported by a pseudo-rational chain of reasoning mixed up with astrological data.

For the founders of iridology, the signs in the iris seemed to reflect an organic state that preceded disease. But when it came to objective criticism, iridology has had to adapt:

> Today it proclaims that these iridal messages do not always show up. They precede the disease, but not always; they are expressed only at certain ages of life and are not permanent. Predisposition is not the obligatory sign of a disease; iridal signs persist after recovery, and there are diseases that are not matched by iridal signs.[4]

These sentences, drawn from one of the bibles of iridology, amount to a proclamation that the diagnosis of a disease does not mean that the disease exists; that the existence of the disease does not necessarily involve the presence of signs in the iris; and moreover that disease is not synonymous with signs.

What are we to think, then, of a diagnostic method that is both inconsistent and liable to induce both negative and positive false readings? For those who believe in iridology, it is not so obvious. They bring into the equation sources borrowed from esotericism, astrology and embryology to defend their territory. For a rational individual, the conclusion is easy: this technique is of no use.

Personally, I prefer a kind of therapy that seems more healthy, to me: reading the work of my friend Henri Broch, *Au Coeur de l'extraordinaire* [*At the heart of the extraordinaire*].[5] He makes mincemeat of the cosmo-esoteric-egypto-astrological delusions and their offshoots, which serve as both the building blocks and the peers of iridology doctrines.

Auriculo-Therapy

Auriculo-therapy (ear acupuncture) is just as popular, and as ill-founded, as iridology. The theoretical bases are identical and the justifications are interchangeable. The same esoteric, astrological, and embryologic sources underlie both practices. Astrology is less influential in auriculo-therapy, but that may be simply because the anatomy of the ear does not lend itself to being cut into sections; but the esoteric and embryologic talk are the same.

Here, the theory is that the outer ear (auricle) is a model of an upside-down fetus, in which various points match up with parts of the patient's body. The ear is checked for tender or sore points, and then an attack on a given organ is treated by acupuncture of the corresponding auricular zone where it is projected. The size of the area covered by the different zones is not proportional to the organ's importance. Thus, the foot is identified precisely, and each toe can be targeted. Conversely, the brain is represented by one tiny spot. But perhaps that is only an empirical observation, related to the size of an auriculotherapist's brain.

Foot Reflexology

If the foot is reproduced in the ear; why shouldn't the ear be projected in the foot? Reflexologists have thus invented the plantar projection of the human body, so that every organ has a corresponding location on the sole (plantar region) of the foot. Reflexology treatment consists of massaging the appropriate zone or stimulating it with an "apple blossom" mallet.

For derivations of the same theoretical bases, the same criticisms hold true.

Given the rate at which we are discovering bodily projections on this or that zone of the organism, quite frankly we can only be optimistic as to the future of such diagnostic and therapeutic methods. Apparently, they have had only two major failures: the projection of testicles onto woman and of ovaries onto man.

8. TASTES AND COLORS

> *A woman was taken for dead, six hours hence. She was ready for burial, when a drop of something brought her back to life and made her stand up and walk about the room.*
>
> Molière,
>
> *A Doctor Despite Himself.*

Chromotherapy

All great traditions use a symbolism of colors in the rites, the ornaments and the outstanding events of life. This symbolism varies with the cultures. Thus white, a color of celebration in the West, becomes the color of mourning in the Orient; while the opposite, red, is an aggressive color in the West but is seen as the color of happiness in the Orient. The symbolism of colors matches up with physical and astrological correspondences, in the Sephiroth of the cabal as well as in the Indian chakras or in hermetic astrology. The astral/color/organ correlation is thus a common denominator to all civilizations: patamedicine could hardly escape it.

Chromo-therapists take color and "administer" it to the patient as a form of treatment. The critical element is to choose a good color, according to the patient's temperament, astral sign and pathology.

The technique consists in catalyzing or dispensing beneficial or malevolent energy by giving the patient a colored light bath. Some chromo-therapists settle for a simple flashlight with colored filters: the "colored vibrations generator" can be applied to the ailing organ, or it can be shined into the patient's pupil so that the energy conveyed by the energy meridians will invigorate the organs concerned. First-class chromo-therapists insist that the patient "be immersed" in a room with monochromatic light, preferably naked, so that the vibrations can penetrate his body.

Such techniques are justified mostly in terms that have to do with traditional magic, even though some chromo-therapists try to provide technical arguments in their favor: society, in its daily activities, has always laid great importance on colors and has established meanings for specific choices — blue for boys and pink for girls, spring green as the color of the hope, etc..

Some chromo-therapists, more imbued with a respect for science, have managed to latch onto certain medical observations and use them to bolster the theoretical bases of their therapy. We know that light plays a role in seasonal depressions: ocular stimulation by sunlight stimulates hormonal secretions in the subject, and they in turn stimulate the production of cerebral neurotransmitters. Therefore, variations in luminosity generate an increase or a reduction in the production of these neurotransmitters; and the subject's psychological state varies with the level of these cerebral neurotransmitters. Thus, the fewer hours of sunshine that we have in the autumn involves a general decline of physiological activity, which precedes the phenomena of depression; in spring, the return of fair weather and longer days is accompanied by a return to the psychological normal.

The human organism's weather-sensitivity explains why some people use artificial light cures to treat depression. Chromo-therapists have picked up these medical observations and adapted them to lend scientific support to their therapy. They have thus produced a list of colors and have spelled out which pathologies or physiological phenomena they are supposed to treat.

Red: must be handled with great care. Revitalizes, aids breathing, increases blood pressure;

Orange: Beneficial. Facilitates pulmonary function, good against boils and carbuncles;

Yellow: Stimulates the nervous system, useful in treating arthritis, mental illness, lymphatic disorders;

Green: A balancing ray, to be used with many precautions. Beneficial in cases of sadness;

Blue: Refreshing, restful. Facilitates expiration and reduces blood pressure, useful in treating asthmas, headaches; helps improve sleep.[1]

Lastly, certain chromo-therapists are happy to market bottles full of colored sand that the patient is supposed to place under her pillow to benefit from beneficial waves that harmonize with her personal energy balance.

Gemstone Therapy and Crystal Therapy

One homeopathic approach uses preparations obtained by trituration (or crushing) of rocks and mineral earths. The list of products on the market sounds like a geological expedition: powdered moonstone, apatite, bauxite, celestite, chalcopyrite, cinnabar, dolomite, feldspar, glauconite, gold, lazulite, limestone, obsidian, pyrolusite, rose sandstone, silver, tournalite. Of these products, uranite is the only one recognized by official medicine.

Treatises on homeopathy are surprisingly discreet, even mum, when it comes to the use of these products — except for limestone, which is prescribed as a calcium supplement. In prescribing these extracts, some homeopaths establish correlations between the ore, the planet that governs it and the astrological sign of the patient.

This technique is nothing compared to the booming business of crystal therapy (crystal work), which is immensely popular with a certain public. It is even taught at the lofty European College of Hypnosis and Natural Medicine. This is a multifaceted practice, in every sense, in which crystals of quartz, amethyst etc. or gemstones are used to "draw light and color into the body's 'aura,' raising its frequency and allowing healthier lower-frequency energies to emerge". This "therapy" is promoted as a treatment for problems as varied as cancer or a poor memory. For lithotherapists (gemstone specialists) and crystal therapists who like traditional mythology, there is an astrological correspondence between the signs of the zodiac, the divinities and the minerals.[2] They frequently make references to mythology and to the Bible.

Other sources refer to the energy action of dolmens and menhirs (standing stones, as at Stonehenge) or to the energy of the pyramids or of meteorites. "Historical" references, however, go as far as quoting from. . . the *Adventures of Tintin*, the popular French storybook. Thus, at a conference in 1997, Dr. Gilbert W. (a dentist), told the story of the diamond of the Temple of Rama to illustrate a stone's energy effect.

> This diamond was stolen from the Temple of Rama by a Frenchman, but the great priests of the temple, in a special ritual, had given the stone consciousness and a negative emotional state in the event of theft — in other words, they attached to it a terrible curse. The seven successive owners of the stone had a series of misfortunes, violent accidents and difficulties — even after diamond was cut in two by an owner seeking to remove the curse from it. The larger half of the diamond was owned by Montespan, then by Louis XVI and Marie-Antoinette (both guillotined), then by an Amsterdam jeweler who was assassinated by his son, and finally by a dethroned sultan, who had it buried with him.

In a time when books on pseudo-Egyptology have started to flourish again, it is no surprise that lithotherapy feeds on themes that resemble the curse of Tutankhamen and the adventures of Indiana Jones.

At any event, lithotherapists say that the stones are equipped with magical and dynamic powers that are supposed to induce in the patient an energy-boosting or a relaxing effect that is psychological as physical. For anyone who might be tempted by this language to give the stones a try, we report below some passages selected from a talk given by a lithotherapist, spelling out which stones have which effects.

Agate: brings self-confidence, good for meditations. Beneficial to all the signs of the zodiac.

Aquamarine: Brings gentle, long-lasting vibrations. It relaxes, helps us learn about the inner self and universal truths, aids communication, and was used by sailors for protection. Brings new ideas, in partnership with the throat chakra. Serves as a talisman for those seeking inspiration. Beneficial to Aquarius, Libra, Gemini and Scorpio.

Obsidian: Strong antidote against negative energies. Makes people focus on what is concrete. Do not meditate with obsidian, for it gives us too much of the truth about ourselves. Do you really want to know the truth? It combats anger. Do not use with children, for it corresponds to the first chakra. Brings general balance. It is not programmable. Suitable for Sagittarius, Capricorn, Aquarius, Cancer, Aries, Scorpio; it interacts with Pluto.

Turquoise: protects all around you by absorbing your own negative thoughts. Protect against the evil eye, and accidents. Brings luck to motorists. The stone of intuition, it brings its own wisdom of communication. If you are ill, it will lose its color and will regain it when you recover. A marvelous gift for the person whom you love; brings as much to the giver as to the receiver. Effective against intoxications, beneficial for all the fluids of the body; protects against poisoning, cholesterol and the effects of sugar. Favorable for the signs of Aquarius, Gemini, Sagittarius, Libra and Scorpio.

Crystal therapy and gemstone-therapy borrow their theories from a melting pot of ideas in which chromotherapy, astrology, and modern medicine are all stirred together, the whole doused with a New Age sauce that enables us to identify the right stone to protect us from auto accidents and broken hearts.

Tele-Therapy

Chromatic tele-therapy is a way of providing long-distance care based on the vibrations of quartz and the iridescent spectrum of cosmic rays. This Oriental therapy, which is little by little taking hold in Europe, does not require the patient to be in the therapist's physical presence. According to the founder, Dr. Batthacharaya (1897 — 1964), tele-therapy works because everything that exists in the universe is composed of the seven colors of the rainbow.

Tele-therapy, like all medical "marvels", has its fables. In 1960, a group of children brought a half-dead cat to Dr. Batthacharaya. The animal had fallen into freezing water. The doctor had the "brilliant intuition" of dangling a crystal pendulum over the animal. After 1,200 rotations, the cat's head and neck lost some of their rigidity; after 3,000 turns, the tail became flexible. Soon the cat was able to walk. After being treated for 15 days with the pendulum, the cat regained its desire to live, and Batthacharaya had the foundations of tele-therapy.

Since swinging a pendulum over a sick organism for several days is no easy job, the new master in tele-therapy built a cardboard booth, with a cardboard disk on top to hold four crystal balls to be moved by the motor from an electric. He repeated his experiment on the next sick cat to come along, and Batthacharaya noted that the cat recovered all its functions after three days of continuous treatment, in spite of having been in a coma for 24 hours. Our inventor then tried one apparatus after another, refining his technique; he replaced the rotating crystal balls with electronic vibrators that would emit rapid flashes of light — colored light coming through prisms.

The ultimate stage in the development of tele-therapy came when Batthacharaya replaced the sick organism (whether cat or human) with a photograph, and subjected the photograph to color vibrations selected according to whatever diagnosis had been made. The diagnosis was reached — needless to say — based on a reading of the colors of the patient's photograph through the prism; any modification of the basic color was the reflection (in both senses of the term) of the disease, and the therapy would aim to restore the chromatic balance of the organism by stimulating the photograph.

The history of tele-therapy does not say whether the technique is effective with instant photographs like Polaroids. In any case, although the founder of tele-therapy has passed away, it is slowly but surely making its way across Europe, seducing fans of chromotherapy and crystal therapy as well as advocates of the Kirlian effect.

9. WAVES AND MAGNETS

Do not imagine that I am an ordinary doctor, just the common run.
Compared to me, all the other doctors are just medical freaks. I have
special talents. I have secrets.

Molière,
The Fleet-Footed Doctor.

The need to explain the inexplicable — the non-reproducible, the unverifiable and the unreal — forces "different" doctors to torn to interpretations based on pataphysics. All the talk about various forms of "energy" becomes a bottomless well into which one can dip at any time, looking for more and more explanations to try to rationalize such and such phenomenon that is presumed to have been observed, or not even observed — only described *ad infinitum*. For this reason, the pallet of the "biological trends" glistens with a thousand hues.

First of all, the energy conveyed by the meridians lines of acupuncture lends a traditional cultural allure to this magical-medical mumbo-jumbo. In this field, practices anchor themselves in history by means of theories on the occult powers or the "gift" of the healer. Dowsing, with its mystical-physics explanations, takes on a hint of science — which can be asserted all the more strongly since a great name in science, Yves Rocard (more about him, below), lent it his unquestionable imprimatur. Wilhelm Reich and his orgone therapy happily recycled the famous tank used by Mesmer — while geo-biology successfully supplements esoteric interpretations of the orientation of how and why cathedrals or pyramids are oriented a certain way.

As for the Kirlian effect, it tries to objectify the mysterious radiations that create the human aura and it seeks to make it possible to work from a photograph to diagnose cancer or the presence of a ghost at a patient's side. Mantras are used in an attempt to create an energy link between the earth and the cosmos while, under hypnosis, the cells of the human body are re-orientated to mount an attack against the disease. Lastly, the waves emitted by crystals and stones are potentialized by those emitted by geometrical forms, and mandalas traced on the body of the patient can repel diseases and demons.

Mesmer and His Bucket

In 1776 Franz Anton Mesmer, a German doctor trained at the University of Vienna, started on the road to riches by disseminating throughout Europe the doctrines of animal magnetism.

Mesmer reckoned that contemporary medical practice was on its deathbed, being unable to solve many fundamental problems. He therefore came to hypothesize the existence of a general energy that must be common to all living beings. According to him, man was united with the universe by a fluid that acted the way magnetism does between two masses of metal. Diseases, then, were the result of poor distribution or a weakening of this fluid.

Just as it is possible to magnetize a metal object by rubbing it against a magnet, so Mesmer thought it must be possible to "reenergize" the individual by plunging him into a universal energy bath.

At first, to effect this "re-energization", he tried hypnotizing his patients (to make them more receptive) and running magnets along their bodies, thus causing a double magnetic effect. Then, having noted that the magnets played only an illusory role, Mesmer gave them up entirely in favor of hypnotic gestures alone.

As his success grew, he soon had to face a tidal wave of patients — up to 200 per day. He then decided to "magnetize" the water
in a pond that ornamented his property, and he began to substitute
footbaths for manually applied magnets. His success grew further. The
authorities of Vienna, unnerved by Mesmerism's popularity, saw it as a
potential factor of social agitation, and Mesmer chose exile in Paris
where caused an identical furor upon his arrival in 1778.

He then decided, with good reason, that footbaths in a goldfish
pond did not project an adequate professional image for him. Moreover, the pond had an unquestionable disadvantage: it was not very
portable. Mesmer thus decided to replace it with the bucket that im-
mortalized him.

> The bucket, or actually a tank, was approximately six to seven feet in
> diameter, and eighteen inches high. It had a double floor, and into the
> space between them he placed items that would conduct electricity,
> including broken bottles, sand, stones, sulphur, and iron filings.
> Then it was filled with water and covered with a floor. The surface of
> the lid was then punctured, some six inches from the perimeter, with
> holes to allow curved iron rods to stick out. The rods were arranged
> in such a way that one end would reach the bottom of the tank, and
> the other could be moved to the patient's stomach, or whichever bod-
> ily part was affected.[1]

This description of the apparatus does not tell us how useful it
was; in truth, the bucket succeeded, in the spirit of its inventor, in fa-
cilitating the circulation of his occult charms between the patients.
This funny kind of group therapy was not conceived with the patient's
welfare in mind, but to save the hypnotist time and energy. It is rather
the meeting place of salutary wills. Mesmer himself did not believe in a
curative power intrinsic to the bucket:

> Alleged imitators of my method have set up in their premises tanks
> that look like the one seen in my treatment room. If that is all they

know, they are not very advanced. It is safe to say that if I had a convenient establishment, I would remove the buckets. In general, I use
such paltry set-ups only when I am forced to do so.[2]

The bucket meetings quickly became a fashionable attraction,
while at the same time they began to spark heated debates. The School
of Medicine took up the issue and suggested that these practices be
banned, stating that some of them qualified as grotesque séances, others as examples of charlatanism, still others — thus demonstrating a
sagacious diagnostic mind — sessions of mass hysteria.

The prohibition of the meetings, at the behest of the School of
Medicine, touched off such an outcry that Louis XVI decided to create
some commissions charged with evaluating the reality of the phenomenon. These commissions were made up of members of the Royal Society of Medicine, on the one hand, and members of the Academy of Science on the other hand. After conducting their investigations and hearings, they returned a mixed report. They acknowledged the reality of
the cures produced, and the impact of Mesmer's techniques, but they
definitively rejected the existence of a possible universal fluid and state
flatly that "animal magnetism" does not exist. Only the botanist Jus-
sieu was convinced, and he asked (fruitlessly) for additional experiments to be conducted. The official interpretation is that the whole
process is a phenomenon of hypnosis, reinforced by the hysterical dynamics that reign in Mesmer groups. Indeed, everyone was mesmer-
ized.

In 1784, the School of Medicine prohibited Mesmer from pursuing
further experiments. He then left France and returned there only occa-
sionally. However, his fans continued to defend his ideas and tried (in
spite of the opposition of the School) to keep them going. One of these
admirers was Abbot Faria, who inspired the character of Alexandre
Dumas' count of Monte-Cristo, Puységur and Delage.

In 1813, Mr. Faria, having just been released after serving a year in
prison, settled in Paris as a hypnotist. After a quick success, he was

soon criticized and caricatured in a satirical play, *Magnetismo-mania*. Called a charlatan by some, a Brahman from the Indies by others (he was born in Goa), he quickly went out of business — but not before he had theorized and described the phenomena of hypnosis by suggestion, in a work entitled *De la cause du sommeil lucide* [*On the cause of lucid sleep*].

In 1826 a report was published; it had been given to the king several years earlier by the astronomer, Bailly. It underlined the "erotic" nature of the Mesmer sessions and the sexual practices observed among those who were most sensitive to the alleged animal magnetism. This report did not prevent Mesmer's disciples (including La Fontaine) from continuing their proselytizing work.

From Mesmerization to Hypnosis

In 1841, James Braid went to one of these Mesmer sessions. A Scottish surgeon enamored of new techniques and doctrines, he was shaken by what he saw, but not convinced. Braid decided to carry out his own investigations. He noted the similarities and the differences between real sleep (which would later be called paradoxical) and hypnotic sleep. He stressed the importance of the phenomena of suggestion in what he then called by the name of critical sleep. He had a presentiment that Mesmerian magnetism was non-existent, and he attempted to set forth the techniques of what would come to be called hypnosis.

He refined a method that consists, for the subject, in staring at a shining point and concentrating on it; he stressed the major role played by suggestibility. Little by little, he provided the foundations of what he called neuro-hypnotism, and later hypnotism. The rupture between Braid and the Mesmerians was complete, after they attacked him in the Mesmerian newspaper *Zoist*, to which Braid responded by publishing *La Physiologie de fascination et critique de la critique* [Physiology of fascination and a critique of criticism].

Little by little, Braid's works entered the canons of mainstream medicine and hypnosis enjoyed wide acceptance, gaining further recognition with Charcot and the Medical School at Salpêtrière.

Mesmerism lingered on, reduced to two basic elements. The first is a theoretical discussion of hypnosis, and the second is the conviction that animal magnetism does not exist and that the phenomena that had been ascribed to it are, instead, the result of a hysterical tendency in the patient. Still, the adherents of universal energy continue their research.

Early in the 20th century, Bose, the famous Indian physicist, was the first to succeed in broadcasting radio waves; he concluded that what amounts to an electric nervous system existed in plants and metals; and he saw it as a form of energy that animated both inorganic nature and living matter. In 1925, the physicist d'Arsonval, member of the French Academy of Sciences, published a report entitled *L'Influence des ondes astrals sur les oscillations des cellules vivantes*. He conducted experiments in partnership with the engineer, Lakhouski, who was perfecting an ultra-short wave apparatus, used with limited success on cancerous tumors. But Lakhouski and d'Arsonval got bogged down in murky theories, trying to describe a universal energy that would explain animal magnetism, dowsing, telepathy, homeopathy and the whole ensemble of manifestations of "planetary energy".

From Kirlian to Rocard

In 1950 Kirlian, a Russian electrician, gave the finishing touches to a process that enabled him to photograph objects with an electric current running through them. Photographs of plants and hands show them surrounded by a kind of halo — pataphysicians see this as the expression of the organism's health, and pataphysicists see it as the revelation of the aura. The Soviets, more materialist than that, saw it as the electrical print of "bioplasm".

But in 1960, animal and human magnetism seemed to regain its lost credit. Professor Yves Rocard, pioneer in radio astronomy, famous nuclear physicist, professor of physics at the elite Advanced Teacher's College, proclaimed loud and clear his conviction that human magnetic phenomena exist. Initially intrigued by the work of a waterfinder (dowser), Rocard sought a logical explanation for this empirical practice. He discovered that "water veins" create geological faults that make local disturbances of the magnetic field. Rocard explained that the waterfinder is not sensitive to the presence of water but to fluctuations in the terrestrial magnetic field — very weak variations, which he estimated to be about $5/1000^{th}$ of the terrestrial magnetic field. For Rocard, the dowser's sensitivity to the magnetic anomaly caused a heightened physiological response in him, with a weakened muscle tone sufficient to cause a noticeable reaction by the rod or pendulum that is the dowser's instrument. The development of proton magnetometers and physiological and anatomical studies prove that some of Rocard's intuitions were accurate.

Today it is thought that the human body may contain magnetite crystals, sensitive to magnetism, like those that are found in the brain of birds and the abdomen of honeybees, enabling them to find the right direction during migrations. Magnetite crystals are also found in the head of dolphins and of many members of the whale family.

Rocard continued his research together with Dr. Baron, director of the laboratory of posturography at the Hospital of Sainte-Anne, in Paris. In spite of some promising experiments claiming to prove the presence of magnetite crystals in the human body (he described six pairs of magnetic sensors: the ankles, knees, elbows, kidneys, neck, and temples), he could not prove definitively that the phenomenon of human magnetism was real. Experiments carried out with dowsers gave inconsistent results that could not be repeated; Yves Rocard thus died without having been able to prove the reality of the phenomenon that he had spent a major part of his research searching for, for nearly thirty years.

Today, French hypnotists and magneto-therapists of all kinds are quick to point to the spiritual heritage of Rocard, taking care not to mention that he had expressed serious reservations over the use of magnets in medicine and that he had concluded — as the true scientist that he was — that one must not draw any final conclusion on the basis of scattered observations that cannot be generalized.[3]

Reich and Orgone

Born in 1897 in Galicia (Austria), Wilhelm Reich[4] studied medicine, then very early became interested in psychiatry; he became the deputy director of the psychoanalytical polyclinic founded by Freud. He soon parted with Freud, with whom he disagreed over the approach to psychoanalytical cures. Reich felt that the therapist must intervene more actively; he should not be satisfied merely to analyze (for his own account and then for the patient) the psychic and body-related data that he gathers.

Along with this criticism, Reich literally became obsessed with the role played by sexual energy in daily life.* His approach, considered to be outrageous and scandalous, caused his professional peers to reject him; he was forced to leave Austria, then Germany, Denmark and Sweden.

In 1934, Reich began experimenting with bioelectricity and in 1936 he came up with vegeto-therapy, which evolved into orgone-therapy, a treatment that proposes to unblock "nodes, tensions and damned-up energy" that correspond to psychic tensions.

In 1937, he set out to study cancer.[5] Having installed himself in the United States, he built the first orgone accumulator and tested it on cancerous mice. The FDA (the U.S. Food and Drug Administration)

---

* Reich believed that "orgones," units of cosmic energy, energized the nervous system. He coined the word on the basis of "orgasm". He considered mental illness to be an orgone deficiency. He leased orgone boxes, in which patients could bathe themselves in the energy field.

soon began inquiring into his work. In spite of the popular success of his ideas and inventions — he made it rain in the desert, thanks to a cloud-buster — he came under increasingly harsh administrative persecution. In 1956, the FDA brought him to trial and his books were burned, his laboratory was destroyed and he was sent to jail, where he died in November 1957.

Orgone. Reich believed that all of creation — and humans, in particular — bathe in a sea of energy: the cosmic orgone. This energy radiates everywhere, and Reich, all his life, would attempt to find it and control it. He built orgone accumulators — big boxes made up of a fibrous matter (intended to retain the radiation) and a metal material (to repel it). In spite of the goodwill of his followers, who gathered together within the Laboratory of Experimental Orgonomy, it seems that no one ever proved the existence of orgone. The limited positive results they achieved have more to do with static electricity or electromagnetic fields than with orgone.

Reich was obsessed with the idea of a linkage between what is biological and what is emotional; and he applied this vision to cancer treatment. For him, cancer patients form were part of a cultural and "ecological" whole. Cancer is the biological expression of emotional and behavioral blockages induced by society, culture, tradition. The patient's psychological block has a corresponding physiological block, which sets off at the cellular level an underdevelopment and an over-oxygenation — which explain the anarchistic growth of cancer cells.

Reich wanted to develop diagnostic and therapeutic methods founded on energy imbalances of orgone. However, it was not his "energy" vision of the nature of human beings that brought down on him the wrath of the anti-fraud squad; it was more his political and economic ideas, and his questioning of the capitalist economic system.

To Reich, all diseases were matters of bioenergetic imbalances — but his orgone apparatuses never proved their effect or the reality of his theories.

Geobiology and Cosmo-Telluric Networks

Attempts to explain the phenomena of dowsing gave rise to theoretical systems freely combining unfounded notions of physics and magic. Geobiology became a favorite playground for those intrigued by "magnetic" interpretations, especially given the endorsement by people like Rocard. Facile extrapolations led to dubious amalgams between medical/scientific knowledge on the one hand and absurd theories on the other hand.

For the geo-biologist, any ailment can stem from an artificial nuisance — electrical pollution, magnetic or cosmic rays, faulty construction materials. But geo-biologists are not satisfied with denouncing natural radioactivity, like that in the granite from Brittany that was used in construction; they go out of their way to highlight subtle forms of pollution like the "memory of the walls", "charged atmospheres", and — why not — "humiliation waves". Consequently, the geobiologist's toolkit is as good as the Ghost Busters'; and it draws its references from a magical and fascinating past.

> Geobiology is both an old and a new science. Indeed, the phenomena it studies have been observed since time immemorial. Places where people felt ill at ease, where they noted health or mental ailments after staying there for a period of time, were regarded as suspect or even cursed. Certain peoples developed methods for "testing" the ground. The Romans grazed their sheep on land that was scheduled for development; after a year passed, they slaughtered the sheep and examined their livers. If anything seemed amiss, the place was regarded as unfit for human habitation. And the American Indians, before establishing a long-term camp, watched how the wild horses in the region behaved; they pitched their tents in the location that the animals preferred.[6]

Needless to say, "medical observations" support the reasoning of our geobiologists.

The first systematic studies on the relationship between environment and health date back approximately a century. Dr. Haviland, in his work *Geography of the Diseases of the Heart, Phthisis and Cancer*, was one of the first to note that cancer did not exist at higher elevations and dry ground, whereas a very strong proportion of this disease could be observed along rivers.

The writings of Dr. Jenny, of Switzerland, are even more spectacular: over a twelve-year period, he tested more than 24,000 mice that had been placed either in a neutral zone or in a geo-pathogenic zone. The first had a normal life and were calm, whereas the second group was very irritable, chewed the screen on their cage, devoured their own young and had a 30% higher incidence of tumors than the animals living in the neutral zone.

Wild imaginings do not hold up over time if they don't have at least a veneer of scientific credibility. Therefore, the geo-biologists built a theoretical arsenal founded on the concept of a cosmo- telluric network — the Hartmann network and the Curry network.

The Hartmann Network:

Scientists have focused on this question of harmful zones and neutral zones, and they have established the existence of a telluric matrix, which has been named for Dr. Ernst Hartmann, who discovered it. It consists of (magnetic) bands that are oriented North-South and East-West, which function like invisible "walls" that are some 21 cm thick. The grid of the network normally forms rectangles which, at our latitude and in an environment that is not too disturbed, have following dimensions: 2 meters in the North-South direction; 2.5 meters in the East-West direction.

The Hartmann network is known as "telluric", for it takes root in the ground and rises vertically, going through dwellings and slabs of reinforced concrete. Its presence has been verified as high as the second level of the Eiffel Tower.

The Curry Network:

> This network was discovered and described in 1952 by Dr. Curry, a German meteorologist. This grid is made up of bands approximately 40 cm broad, and is oriented at a diagonal to the Hartmann network.

> When a Curry band crosses an intersection on the Hartmann network, this zone is particularly active. If intersections of both networks happen to coincide and are superimposed, then we have a zone that is even more active. If one or other network happens to be superimposed over a fault, a watercourse or a spring, etc., that point will be particularly active.

These networks are reckoned to affect human health, and the geobiologists extended their competence to a new patascience: the "medicine of the habitat", which aims to cure disturbances induced by a poorly situated bed, water pipelines, or the house more generally.

> Certain forms of heating and air-conditioning systems encourage the destruction of negative ions — whereas ions improve, among other things, the operation of the endocrine system. In parallel, this modern comfort causes the positive ions to multiply, and they contribute to weakness and various disorders. Current building techniques: slabs of reinforced concrete, metal girders — themselves generate magnetic fields that influence the people who live in these buildings; and let's not forget poorly grounded electrical circuits and grounding stakes that happen to be located on a "geopathogenic" point.

And so, geobiologists not only sell their services, they market detection equipment: "lobe-antennas", "parallel rods", "wave detectors" of every kind, derived from the voltmeter and ammeter but sold, you may be sure, at hefty prices.

Since there is no point in getting your home diagnosed if you aren't going to follow through with treatment, the geo-biologist will propose that his client to plant para-waves poles, to lay cables to cut the networks, to change how his bed is oriented bed or to move the drain-pipes, even to sell his house and emigrate to a piece of land that is less noxiously charged. It is a safe bet that the sacrifice made by the client will not be in vain — it will serve to enrich an understanding real estate agency that is willing to take on the selling of this home, despite its harmful and phantom waves. Don't give up hope — sometimes it is possible to purify your home, with the help of a qualified geo-biologist, who will teach you how to reduce chemical pollution by using non-toxic paint and varnishes.

> The geobiologist can also act on disturbances that are of more subtle origin (let us say of a less "material" nature): for instance, a "cosmo-telluric" flare can be moved if it runs into your dwelling. As for the "memory of walls and charged objects" (i.e. the trace of events from the past, sometimes long past), or the "psychic residues" left by earlier occupants, techniques of purification and "subtle" cleansing must be used; they are supposed to improve the place's vibrational rhythm.

Magnetized Radishes and Spermatozoids

These magnetists and hypnotists do not shy away from any sacrifice, and no living thing, vegetable or animal, escapes their power. Magnetism is supposed to increase plants' growth and fruit-bearing; and it is a universal therapy.

> Peas and radishes sprout better when they are under to the influence of a magnetist. This was proven in September-October 1984 in the service of one of our most eminent cancer specialists, at the hospital Paul-Brousse de Villejuif.

> Pots were sown with pea and radish seeds and were divided into two

groups: one watered with ordinary water, the other with water that had been treated for ten minutes by the magnetist.

Result: in the pots that were watered with plain water, 60% of the plants grew to between 10.5 and 16.5 cm. In the pots where "magnetized" water was used, 84.6% of the plants grew to that height. A statistically significant result, according to the specialists. The conclusion: magnetism exists.

As for the therapeutic power of magnetism, Jean-Paul Escande reports on it, humorously, in *Mirages de la médecine*.

An innkeeper in Villeneuve who worked as a healer in his off-hours, Réné S., 44 years old, was a devotee of soft, even tender, medicine. His reputation spread beyond the county. A patient from the town of Lot came to consult with the magnetizer, and in all confidence agreed to undergo the treatment recommended by this "doctor".

"My dear young lady, you are not suffering from breast cancer, but from a uterine fibroma!" And he explained in detail how a cure could be achieved: "You can only be treated with magnetized spermato-zoids, as they will attack the sick cells. . ." Since the magical spermatozoids were not immediately available, the good doctor offered to sacrifice his own little cells, for the moderate sum of eighty francs per session. . . weekly!

The treatment ended up going on for a long time. The young woman, with good cause, did not feel any better. The magnetist insisted that he did not dare to stop the cure. Stopped it was, and brutally, by the wife of the innkeeper, who one day surprised the magnetist and pa-tient in full consultation. The patient, her eyes finally opened, filed suit for rape.[7]

10. CANCER, AIDS AND ETERNAL YOUTH

If all these fake medical practices had been satisfied with offering cures for hay fever and chronic constipation, they might be silly, but their harm probably would have remained limited. However, they claim to be useful in a field that is far more vast, and their preferred targets are very serious illnesses.

Patamedicine grows and thrives, today, in the field of cancer and AIDS treatment. In this branch of industry, it valiantly resists objective criticism. It has, indeed, a wonderful opportunity to point out that it cannot succeed across the board where traditional medicine often fails, and it takes advantage of the patient's fear, as he is ready to go into debt in the hope of being cured or at least of surviving.

In this particular field of health, for a whole century, the most cynical swindlers have blended with inventive people working in good faith, which makes it even harder for patient and expert alike to choose a course of treatment, since they are often taken in by the miraculous spiel of these modern Fausts.

When it comes to AIDS and cancer, miracle treatments and therapeutic machines have proliferated for fifty years.

Niehans and Young Cells

With a series of lawsuits and a stream of impassioned declarations, Dr. Niehans made headlines in the forensic world for close to two decades.

In about 1930, this Swiss surgeon asserted, on the basis of his observations, that he had just discovered a new technique that slows down ageing, stimulates tissues and fires up the organs by accelerating their functions; this effect was created by injecting fresh cells taken from similar organs in a fetus or young animal — primarily sheep and bovines. He also considered placental injections to be promising, in terms of rejuvenation. Niehans proclaimed that injections of liver cells, spleen, pancreas, bone marrow or sexual organs could revitalize his patients.

The fresh cells must be injected within forty minutes of their having been extracted from the animal, according to Niehans, in order to avoid allergic phenomena that he ascribes to the "rejection response" to dead cells. The Niehans cure thus justified the opening of several centers for specialized care; the most famous being the clinic "La Prairie", in Montreux, Switzerland. Cell-therapy claims to treat hormonal dysfunctions as well as ageing and psychiatric disorders — schizophrenia, depression, and even mongolism.

In spite of the absence of clinical observations that could objectively confirm the improvements or supposed healings that are claimed, cellular therapy quickly developed a following. However, it is being criticized more and more sharply, as healings give way to complications, most frequent of which are allergic reactions, cutaneous eruptions, joint problems and changes in diseases that are as different as tuberculosis and encephalopathy. Since 1959, there have been several deaths following cellulo-therapy sessions. The blame for three deaths in 1987, including that of a young German decathloner, has been laid squarely on cell-therapy.

In France, this practice was banned in 1956, but it continues to be practiced illegally behind the discreet doors of certain medical offices. The current price of an ampoule of freeze-dried cells is close to $200, and the cure is supposed to require some 12 to 30 ampoules. However, the use of cellular extracts has benefited from the newly enforced Europe-wide jurisprudence, which has ruled that it is against the European directives to forbid the use and marketing of these products in France. Decrees dated March 7, 1989 and April 8, 1992, from the European Community Court of Justice, thus considered it to be "contrary to articles 30 and following, of the Treaty of Rome, the prohibition on private individuals' importing drugs in quantities not exceeding the normal personal needs of a patient". Article L601-2 of the Code of Public Health, modified on May 28, 1996 henceforth authorizes "a patient and a doctor to use, on an exceptional basis, . . . a drug prescribed . . . to the patient by name . . . under the responsibility of his attending practitioner, when its effectiveness and safety are presumed in the current state of scientific knowledge and it is likely to show actual benefit".

In the absence of serious clinical studies, and riding the wave of media-medical hype that had surrounded the Niehans method for helf a century, some none-too scrupulous doctors import (or have their patients import), freeze-dried products that in fact bear little relationship to those promoted by Niehans — but which at least are bacteriologically harmless.

Never proven either effective or harmless, cell-therapy is very popular in Germany and gained an avid following in France, in spite of a center being closed in 1993 and its director sent to jail.

Mad cow epidemics and the problems arising from genetic engineering have not, to date, been enough to turn off the proponents of this method, which not incidentally represents a considerable source of revenue for certain "specialized" experts, some of whom also supply steroids etc. to athletes.

The Aslan Cure, Gerovital

Under the Ceausescu regime, Romania developed what was, at the very least, an original source of foreign currency by promoting the work of Dr. Anna Aslan. Coupled with spa treatments given at the seaside resorts along the Adriatic coast, this method consisted in administering procaine via injection; its promoters called procaine an aid to cellular rejuvenation.

Marketed under the name of Gerovital, Gerovital H3 or LD 40, procaine is at first a vasodilator (dilating the blood vessels), which briefly improves capillary circulation — an improvement quickly followed by a rebound effect in the form of increased vasoconstriction.

Along with the vasoconstriction/vasodilatation phenomenon is accompanied by a modification of the rate of heartbeat, whose effect is immediately perceived by the followers of the method. However, while this braking/accelerating effect creates a kind of excitation and a euphoric effect for the patient, there are more disadvantages than advantages — for it subjects the organism (generally middle-aged or older) to physiological jolts without long-term benefit.

After the death of Anna Aslan and the fall of the Ceausescu regime, the Aslan or Gerovital cure slipped out of sight before gradually reappearing in Germany, the United States and again in Romania. These days, it is gradually taking hold in France, where it is found under the name of the Aslan Cure, or as an additive to rejuvenation cures recommended by spas and specialized treatment centers. There is also a kind of under-the-table market in Gerovital ampoules, and there is every reason to think that, since history suffers from chronic amnesia, the Aslan cures soon will become again a source of hard currency for seaside resorts along the Black Sea, the Dalmatian coast . . . and maybe the Atlantic.

Dr. Vernes's Aqueous Solutions

Variations in blood serum provide the bases of a diagnostic technique and a therapeutic method perfected by Dr. Arthur Vernes.

Born in 1879 into a family of Protestant bankers, young Vernes had his medical studies interrupted by an attack of tuberculosis that immobilized him for several years. Thus, as soon as he finished boarding school, he turned toward traditional research on tuberculosis, and syphilis, which was having a devastating impact early in the 20th century. As a hospital laboratory director, he developed a method of analysis extrapolated from the photometer invented by Arago for use in physics.

Vernes's diagnostic technique entailed taking blood samples from the patient and isolating the serum, then distributing it in small glass containers, and subjecting it to light rays. Adjusting the dilution rate of the serum in the containers, Vernes observed that the diffused light varied according to the concentration but that the variations were not linear — sometimes the variations were sudden and marked. He discovered that at certain rates of dilution, fine particles appear, suspended in the liquid, blocking the light. And he noted, finally, that the light spectra obtained using serum from healthy subjects was different from those of sick patients. This led him to conclude that light profiles might correspond to specific diagnoses and might reflect changes in the patients' conditions. According to Vernes, these light profiles make it possible to give diagnoses, and also to minutely monitor the effects of the treatment.

Going further along the same theoretical trajectory, Vernes elaborated a form of treatment calling for the use of light-treated metals. Vernes' products were marketed for some thirty years with the blessing of the French government, and were reimbursable by the public health administration, just as some homeopathic specialties enjoy state support today. In 1981, an inspection by the pharmaceutical administration discovered that the masterly Vernes preparations, supposedly made up individually for each patient on the basis of the patient's own test results, were in fact produced industrially according to standard formulas. Following this revelation, the Vernes products were withdrawn from the list of the reimbursable products and lawsuits were filed for fraudulent advertising.

Cancerometry. The Vernes method of cancer diagnosis, or cancerometry, is an outgrowth of a series of blood analyses (especially the flocculation of blood with acidified copper acetate) that he refined in about 1920 and used, at that time, to test patients' blood for tuberculosis and syphilis. Some of these tests have been, if not improved, then at least modified, on the basis of enhancements in laboratory assaying techniques.

Cancerometry is supposed to be a powerful enough tool to not only diagnose cancer but also to follow its course.

However, the Vernes method, while it represented an advance in the history of biological diagnosis, today is completely obsolete (as the Academy of Medicine has affirmed on several occasions). In fact, these days cancerometry is to biological diagnosis what cauterization is to surgery.

Upon Vernes's death, in 1976, the cases being covered at the institute he had founded in Paris in 1916 were picked up by the Villejuif hospital. Vernes's *postmortem* drama is that his method has been discredited by the proponents of alternative medicines, who offer it as a reliable means of tracking cancer and verifying that the treatment is working. This discredit reflects onto Vernes himself, who, during his lifetime, had managed to change with the times; but his heritage has been co-opted by medical neanderthals.

Moreover, no experimentation has ever proved the effectiveness of the administration of metals and metallic oligosols applied according to the Vernes method.

Physiatrons

Synthetic physiatrons — wonder drugs for the pains associated with cancer — were marketed by Jean Solomidès for thirty years before they were banned. They still have not disappeared completely from the black market.

The mystery that surrounded the production and marketing of these products bears a striking resemblance to that of the Beljanski products[1] today. It is this mystery that enables these products — generally of quite ordinary, if not dangerous, composition — to sell at high prices. If we knew what went into such a product, we would not be willing to pay for it, and we would also realize that it cannot be effective. And that would be bad for business.

On December 18, 1978, Dr. Solomidès was arrested for illegal practice of medicine and pharmacy; his institute was shut down and he was fined. He died on June 28, 1979, so the criminal trial was closed, but the Solomidès affair lived on through his beneficiaries. On July 28, 1983, a new investigation was started; and when the institute was searched, all the equipment for producing the Solomidès products was seized. At the same time, the government asked the police prefect to shut down the entire establishment, since "tests conducted by the National Health Laboratory on samples taken from the institution [have] shown the products in question to be toxic".

These analyses revealed that the synthetic physiatrons marketed by Solomidès's widow in fact contained testosterone, quinine and citral-urethane — a fact that had been known for nearly ten years by those who had gone to the trouble of considering using this treatment. Because citral-urethane is considered a poison, the production of physiatrons was banned, leading to a feud between the defenders of Solomidès and the defenders of medical legality. The legal eagles once more demonstrated that peremptory rigor that reinforces the paranoia of the others, but did not dim the enthusiasm of Solomidès's fans. Prohibition in itself is not accepted as proof (fair enough) that something does not work or is dangerous.

What Can the Medical Establishment (or Government) Do?

As has so often been the case, the Solomidès scandal illustrated the inability of the medical establishment and the government — and the defenders of medicine that really works — to defuse the phenomena of mindless enthusiasm that surrounds pseudo-medicine. Medical hoaxes are born every day, and more and more seminars and conferences promote their techniques; meanwhile, practitioners of official medicine usually settle for publishing laconic official statements on the danger of such and such technique, without offering any proof. In this way, they are no better than the apostles of alternative medicine, whom they condemn for not proving their points with scientific tests and demonstrations. Consequently, when a procedure or treatment is banned, it takes on the allure of the forbidden, and gives the con artists the luster of added credibility.

Every time a supposedly new and groundbreaking technique is condemned by official medicine, it sets off a persecution complex among the technique's defenders. The inventor of the technique gains prestige — he becomes the Messiah, the one with answers, holder of wisdom — that official medicine and its minions (government officials, police chiefs, judges) want to keep quiet. The defenders of patamedicine are remarkably better at lobbying and using the media than are their counterparts in traditional medicine. Often, court decisions are scientifically justified but are not explained in sufficient detail; they only end up giving a boost to the illusory product or technique, promoting it more effectively to potential consumers than its own followers can do.

Fighting against medical charlatanism means, above all, explaining and explaining again, spelling things out, making it clear to the patients that such techniques may or may not produce the advertised effects, that a technique may succeed in laboratory testing but still may not necessarily work for the patient, and that such and such biochemical effect, even if it is experienced as advertised, is not necessarily the sign of a physiological healing action.

Many are the cases that illustrate this deficiency of communication. In the case of the Solomidès synthetic physiatrons, the officials should have taken the time to explain that they were prohibited not only because the components were toxic, but also because of the absence of any real clinical trials that might have proven both the effectiveness of the treatment and its long-term harmlessness for the patient.

Indeed, some experiments have been conducted in an effort to prove the effectiveness of the Solomidès products, but they are unconvincing, for two reasons:

- they were carried out *in vitro* on isolated cells, which is absolutely not proof that the product works in the context of a human organism;
- the tests that were conducted on individual patients were carried out on too small a sample to be persuasive.[2]

The patamedicine lobby includes spin-masters highly accomplished in the art of publishing and distributing "white papers" intended to reveal a plot on the part of the great pharmaceutical companies, the medical Mafia and the Government to prohibit a certain technique that is supposed to be THE definitive solution to medical problems. The authorities who are responsible for maintaining public health must stop leaving themselves exposed to this criticism from the followers of patamedicine and should publish in their turn articles and papers exposing these endless hoaxes. In this period that is so critical for the future of the health care system, when the chaotic proliferation of forms of care and types of organizational structures is giving way to a more constraining set-up, it becomes fundamentally important to give the consumers precise information in the field of medicine.

Given the debate over how the role of the State and the insurance companies in the health care system, given our growing anguish as we recognize the limits of medicine, the patient may be tempted to take refuge in illusory paradises maintained by the special interest groups promoting fake natural health remedies. The preventive campaigns ("Don't Smoke!", "Use a Condom!") are more like recruitment slogans than real information, and can hardly be expected to make a dent in this problem. And when medical decisions are delegated to bean-counters and government bureaucrats, it certainly does not help get the ship back on course.

The Beljanski Scandal

The revelation that French President François Mitterrand had cancer touched off a debate that actually had its roots some fifteen years earlier. The president was supposedly one of the recipients of a miracle drug produced by Mirkos Beljanski. Is that truth or rumor? We will never really know for sure.

At the end of the 1980's, the holding company Abraxas, gave Professor Jean Cahn a product to test, to verify whether it was effective against the AIDS virus.[3] According to the professional opinions given by Prof. Andrieu, Director of the Tumor Immunology Laboratory at the Laennec Hospital in Paris, and by Dr. Chantal Damais, Research Director at INSERM, the tests showed "remarkable" results, and according to the experimenters the product, *in vitro*, inhibited the release of Interleukin 6 by white blood cells from seropositive patients. In spite of these promising results, Beljanski never got clearance from the French equivalent of the FDA to bring his products to market. On the contrary, Beljanski refused any study that might have been able to assess fairly the viability of his products.

Born in 1923, Mirkos Beljanski received a doctorate in biology in 1948. He joined the prestigious Pasteur Institute, where he worked in Dr. Lépine's laboratory to develop a polio vaccine. A few years later, he started working with Dr. Monod and dropped his research on DNA and its function. After Monod, Lwoff and Jacob won the Nobel Prize in medicine in 1965, Beljanski was upset with his former colleagues and left the Pasteur Institute. He then took a job as research director in the Pharmacy School of Châtenay-Malabry. And at that time he devoted his applied research to cancer, in particular, and then to AIDS.

In 1983, Beljanski made waves by marketing a product that claimed to restore the percentage of white blood cells in a patient's blood. This product was presented by the patamedical press as a wonder drug for desperate cases, such that of young Valerie, an eleven year old, who was cured of medullary aplasia after treatment with BRL (Beljanski Remote Leucocyte). Fifteen years later, BRL has not, to our knowledge, had any major medical repercussions — which is astonishing, for a drug of such a great importance.[4]

After retiring in 1988, Beljanski holed up in a garage that he baptized with the pompous title of the Center for Biological Research (CERBIOL). From this facility he put the finishing touches on various products, which were marketed illicitly through the intermediary of a company named Cobra. For nearly fifteen years, while apparently-promising laboratory results were being published, Beljanski refused to reveal the composition of his products and refused to submit to the formal testing required by the authorities in order to secure product approval. As is true for so many other substances, the results produced by Beljanski products during *in vitro* experiments cannot be extrapolated to the living individual, and Beljanski's products never proved that they work *in vivo*.

Little by little, Beljanski and his team started to act like they were under siege, and started promoting a set of paranoiac themes. Beljanski became the "persecuted researcher", attacked by the multinational drug companies and maligned by the medical authorities. The Health Minister came down hard on the Beljanski products in a press release dated August 27, 1990.

> On the scientific level ... one can only express the utmost reservation over the claims Beljanski makes. The proof of quality, safety and effectiveness required of any drug before it can be brought to market cannot, indeed, be replaced by personal testimonies and a few non-controlled test cases.

> A special task force was set up at my request to study this case, and to accelerate the study of proposed therapies for these diseases. The cases of 27 patients being treated for HIV infection were studied for more than three months, and did not show any effect. No file concerning patients suffering from cancer was addressed by Mr. Beljanski.

The Cobra Association changed its name to The Outstretched Hand, while Beljanski was welcomed by Patriarch, which financed his research and helped him gain access to the necessary population of HIV-positive individuals. Whatever the value of Beljanski's work, this alliance is shocking. "If you dine with the devil, be sure to use a long-handled spoon."

As a footnote, on October 27, 1998, Fate handed down a final judgment, proving beyond any reasonable doubt that Beljanski's method does not work. At the age of 74, Mirkos Beljanski passed away, in the quiet of his home in Paris, from cancer.

11. From Mother Ocean to the All-Embracing Mother

What would we be, then, without the aid of that which does not exist?
Myths are the souls of our actions and our loves.
We can only act by hurling ourselves toward a phantom.
We can only love that which we create.
  Paul Valéry.

Tcharkovski's Baby Dolphins

Every event that takes place, whether on some corner of our planet or in the space that surrounds it, as long as it gets a bit of media coverage that presents it one day under a favorable light, is likely to serve as a catalyst for an acceleration or a revival of the mythical aspirations of various fringe groups.

Thus, when the comet Halle-Bop passed close to Earth, the millenarist and apocalyptic groups stepped up their activity. Similarly, when Roswell's dopey story about extraterrestrials was shown on TV, it revived the interest of groups that believe in UFO's. Lastly, every discovery in Egyptology sparks the interest of the esoterists who believe all kinds of things in regard to the great pyramid. Sometimes, a movie plays this role. When *Grand Bleu* came out, based on the life of Jacques Mayol, it moved many young people to an intense longing for the lonely depths of the sea and inspired part of the population to begin to identify with the dolphin, star of the film.

Not content with being *sapiens*, man brutally discovered that he was *aquaticus*. The chimpanzee was no longer his ancestor — the sweet little dolphin took its place, the dolphin with whom we suddenly felt we shared genes and wished to share the oceanic life, with all its consequences.

On June 16, 1990, a little after sunrise — a mythical moment — a human baby was born at a depth of five feet. This marine labor was the latest in a series that had begun a few years earlier and had won over certain forward-looking maternity wards, most of which have since closed down. The Tcharkovski method, was unfurled with much hoopla and was soon on TV all over France. Master Tcharkovski having remained in Guinea, one of his disciples, Katia Bagsianski, led the crusade to spread the good word. The Tcharkovski theory is based on a relatively simple, not to say simplistic, postulate. As the intra-uterine life of the fetus takes place in a watery milieu — amniotic fluid — the purpose of underwater birthing is to mitigate the enormous shock to the baby that his first contact with universe of dry air represents. This technique is similar to the one that was already being practiced in private clinics in warm water pools.

> In France, underwater birthing came to us thanks to Dr. Michel Odent, who practiced it in the maternity of the hospital of Pithiviers until 1985. What made Odent unique is that he places great importance, in the preparation of the future mothers, on relaxation sessions in warm water (and not in icy water). It is a technique of psycho-physiological training more than a technique of labor. When the first contractions take place, the birthing mother takes refuge at first in the soft liquid ambiance. Most of them come out of the water at the last moment; and the child comes into this world in the open air. According to Odent, the thermal shift between the warm water and the external air sets off a secretion of hormones — adrenalin and endorphins — which facilitates the final effort. Some women go through labor in a standing position, clutching the edge of the swimming pool. Some of them (a minority) stay in the water until the end. The child is then born into the liquid element; he is quickly brought up to the surface, and is given the same care as those who are born in the air.[1]

The Tcharkovski method was supposed to be even more powerful, since the birth took place in a saline (sea water having nearly the same salinity as that of human plasma) and natural milieu (in the open water, so that the cosmic waves can penetrate the marine waves unobstructed, through the cosmo-telluro-marine vector represented by the medium Tcharkovski or one of his assistants).

Television then broadcast the documents provided by Tcharkovski and his disciples, often together with flattering comments. Images were shown, including sequences filmed in Moscow in winter, with an outdoors temperature of -15C.° While Tcharkovski's assistants are tightly wrapped in coats and fur hats, the newborn child is immersed in a basin covered with ice. The participants comment — in all conviction — that the child is protected by the cosmic waves that the Master, Tcharkovski, and his disciples generate by establishing a magnetic cordon around the hole dug in the ice. Other documents show Katia Bagsianski herself, in labor, squatting in the frozen water of the Black Sea. After keeping the child in the water for a few moments, she brings it out, shakes it by holding it by the head, and cuts the umbilical cord. There is also a document showing a woman in labor following this technique, in a squatting posture, on the coast of Corsica — at a temperature that was, fortunately, more forgiving.

The Tcharkovski method has some disciples in France, and periodically it comes back into vogue thanks to some enlightened obstetrician who wants to drum up business by mentioning his name.

Tcharkovski founded his technique on two theoretical justifications.

1. He suggested that it would lessen the shock of birth by adding a transitory stage between the comfort of the womb and the harsh external environment;

2. This is supposed to keep the child longer in contact with a dolphin — his dolphin. Tcharkovski said that every human

being has a dolphin guardian that looks over him and commu-
nicates with him all his life. The death of the dolphin causes
energy disturbances for the human, which leads to disease,
and vice versa.

The esoteric justifications offered by Tcharkovski are not very
convincing, to a rational mind. For the upholders of traditional medicine, they do not count for much when compared with the complications this method can cause. The recommended transition may, indeed,
ease the stress on the fetus, but that has never been proven, even when
the labor takes place in a warm aqueous milieu.

On the other hand, there can be many complications:

- the birth may take longer, thus adding to the risk of oxygen
  deprivation to the brain of the newborn baby, which can entail
  massive neurological complications up to and including quadriplegia and major cerebro-motor handicaps;
- septic complications are frequent, causing various infections
  for the child as well as for the mother, in particular due to fecal
  germs from the mother, which are dispersed in a milieu that
  favors bacterial development;
- thermal shock, in the case of sea births at cold temperatures,
  can cause a deregulation of the internal temperature with
  complications such as cerebral hemorrhage, enterocolite ne-
  crosis, cardiac disorders;
- finally, one very ordinary complication can occur: the newborn
  can drown.

For specialists in obstetrics and neonatal medicine, the Tcharkovski technique offers no benefits to the baby, even if it is more com-
fortable for the mother.[2]   Indeed, underwater birthing does provide
more comfort for the mother, who is supported by the water. It pre-
vents dorsal decubitus, which impedes uterus-placenta circulation.

Thus, in some civilizations, the mother gives birth in a squatting position, which facilitates expulsion.

By contrast, being born in water offers no advantage for the newborn. The fetus lives in a perfectly adapted hydrous environment which is not matched, in any event, by the new environment; and water birth only briefly prolongs this stay which has to be interrupted anyhow, so that the child can adapt to the air environment that is his. Artificially prolonging the stay in water, in addition to the already stated complications, can cause an interruption of placenta/newborn circulation and can cause oxygen deprivation that may go unrecognized. For, giving birth this way means that there can be no effective medical supervision — monitoring, for example.

It is troubling to see patients who are convinced that the Tcharkovski technique is based on cogent reasoning and who support it using the argument that it is "natural". Man — and woman — are air animals, and even if our gestation takes place in a "watery" milieu like all mammals, we have undergone a several-million-year evolution that has led us to a form of labor that is similar to that of all mammals — except the delphides and the whales. So one has to wonder why anyone would be interested in a phylogenetic regression and the bio-mystical arguments that support it.

Neonatal Memories

All sorts of charlatans have found a thriving market in the notions surrounding bogus claims about neonatal and prenatal memories, and better yet, past life recall. Neonatal suffering is also used as argument to sell psychoanalytical care. L. Ron Hubbard and his Scientologists play on this, preaching a technique of "auditing" that they claim will dissolve the psychic "engrams" that disturb the subject. But the market is so vast that no one can monopolize it, and the myth of birth memories crops up in pseudo-medical and pseudo-scientific periodicals on a regular basis.

> Traumatic birth carves very strong memories into the mind/body system, memories that many people think cause or encourage disease.
>
> Once, while traveling by ship, Dr. David Cheek (an obstetrician and hypnotist from Chico, California) met another passenger who had severe headaches. He had suffered for years, always on the right side, above the eye. Dr. Cheek hypnotized him and took him back to the moment of his birth, to find out the cause of the headaches.
>
> The man told the story of a violent birth. He felt his head squeezed by a sharp pain, above the eye, on the face and in the back of the neck. Dr. Cheek thought that it might have been an attempt to facilitate a difficult birth, using forceps.
>
> When it was time to disembark from the ship, the doctor met the passenger's mother, who confirmed that the birth had been traumatic indeed, and involved a desperate use of forceps at the last moment.
>
> Remembering a difficult labor, under hypnosis, is often all it takes to relieve migraines and chronic headaches.[3]

This type of wild imagining, which ignores the essential facts of neurology, physiology and obstetrics, leads to more and more absurd conclusions that are used to support the theories of many quack physicians and healing cults.

The above-cited article goes on in the same vein, and we discover that cells have their own memory. (Why not, after all, if water has its own memory?) We learn that Caesarean birth creates anxiety in the child by depriving it of a physical and psychological pleasure, that a child born in this way does not know his bodily proportions, and that he will have a need to be caressed and listened to, throughout his sexual life. Any pinching of the umbilical cord during birth is not, they say, dangerous to the child, but can create stress and anxiety in the adult, or throat problems if it happened that the umbilical cord got wrapped around the neck. Lastly, according to this article, when a placenta gets in the way it causes psychic difficulties that can be as severe as schizophrenia and antisocial conduct.

These delusions form the foundation of the most dangerous and obscure techniques:

> Not only hypnosis but psychotropic drugs can be used to stimulate memories of the moment of birth. Dr. Grof has used LSD and other drugs on thousands of patients to help them remember pre-birth traumas and thus confront them and work them through.

> Dr. Tcharkovski developed a new method of underwater birthing. The result of this means of giving birth without gravity has spawned a new generation of "superbabies", with memories of very happy birth. The children are much better and have a far higher intelligence quotient than the average for their age group, giving them many advantages in school. These children are also psychologically superior: they are happier, more sociable and have a more peaceful temperament.[4]

And there are other techniques, playing on the concept of a happy birth, that find some receptivity in a society that is somewhat poor in miracles, myths and poetic fantasies.

The Tomatis Method

Alfred Tomatis heads the list of experts who have found a way to take advantage of all these fantasies that surround our birth. A former ear-nose-throat specialist, he was thrown out by the medical authorities in 1977.

Tomatis played perfectly on the guilt feelings of parents and future parents, as Bruno Bettelheim had done a few years before. Tomatis left no room for doubt: the baby recognizes the voice of the mother (and father), heard during the "long uterine night" that preceded the labor. He went on to elaborate a theory on the psycho-emotional disturbances of children and their relationship to the sound disturbances to which they were subjected during gestation, in particular focusing on such things as vocal outbursts during arguments, and the consecutive modifications of language in states of stress.

Tomatis maintained that, starting in the first months of pregnancy, the fetus is sensitive to the sounds coming from outside, mainly the voice of his or her mother, transmitted through the uterine and placental barrier. After having reconstituted what he calls the "acoustic impressions" of the fetus, using filtered sounds recorded in water, Tomatis has young children listen to these montages of sound, thereby conducting what he calls "sonic labor".

This technique was never persuasive to music-therapists and specialists in electro-acoustics, who point out (correctly) that the voice is muffled by the filter of the amniotic liquid combined with the various tissues that separate the fetus from the airspace where voluntary maternal sounds are created (her voice, and song).

Moreover, Tomatis skips over the issue of sound "parasites" that disturb the hypothetical fetal listening: the sound of heart beats, digestion, cracking joints, and muscular rustlings that make up the aural environment of the fetus.

Neither does he address the arguments of his former professional colleagues, who have pointed out to him that the ear of the fetus is blocked with a mucous plug that only disappears after birth.

He defies the criticisms of the neurophysiologists who counter his beautiful theories with the fact that, since the nervous system is not yet mature, it is difficult to understand how already muffled sound impulses can make their way to an incompletely-formed brain through incomplete nervous connections.

Despite all that, Tomatis's theories have managed to gain a following among the general public and part of the medical world. It is true that they are based on his personal interpretation of work carried out by the acoustic laboratory of physiology of Port-Royal. These experiments aim at proving that the fetus is sensitive to sound frequencies ranging between 800 and 2000 hertz, when these frequencies are played through the abdominal wall using a speaker placed on the mother's belly. The sound from the speaker is transmitted by the vibration of the abdominal wall, which acts as a resonator. But they don't talk about the fact that the sound environment is not limited to these frequencies — far from it; that the voice human represents only a tiny part of the sound environment; and future mothers find walking awkward enough without having speakers strapped to their bellies.

What really brought fame and fortune to the Tomatis method is that it uses a unique apparatus: the electronic ear. This is an apparatus that filters the sound of the maternal voice, and music, cutting out deeper frequencies and emphasizing higher tones above eight thousand hertz.

The Tomatis treatment is intended for children who are autistic or emotionally disturbed, those with speech difficulties, behavioral problems, or learning disabilities. The treatment consists in listening to the mother's voice, filtered — such as it is supposed to have been heard by the fetus during gestation. The objective is to bring the child back to the pre-natal period in order to encourage training in total listening. After a first stage of listening to the filtered maternal voice, the child is subjected to sessions of listening to filtered music, alternating with sessions of language acquisition, then with sessions copied from more traditional speech therapy.

The program is divided into two principal parts:

In the first phase, the child receives auditory stimulation, using a helmet and a vibrator. Music is used as the initial stimulus and will be gradually filtered to reproduce the sonic universe corresponding to the process of listening as it was before birth.

If any positive results follow a Tomatis treatment, that is obviously due to the closer attention and intensive training given to the young children, to the traditional speech therapy sessions, and to the psychological acceptance of responsibility — and not to the electronic ear, as the Tomatis documents implicitly acknowledge:

> The monitoring sessions. . . are for taking stock — with the child, alone or accompanied by his/her parents. The session is a time for evaluating the progress that has been made. This is an occasion for the child to express his experiences and his reactions.

> The consultant explains to the child what is happening, and advises the parents so that the family climate becomes increasingly harmonious and thus contributes to the blossoming of the child's personality.

Tomatis wanted to make his technique universally applicable, and that is precisely what reveals the manipulative aspect of his efforts. The electronic ear was supposed to resolve all difficulties of communication, psychological problems, delays in language and social development — it was even supposed to improve the vocal performances of singers!

While his magic ear may have seduced the public, Tomatis failed in his attempt to develop a theoretical framework, because it rested on a foundation of untruths. According to him, the right ear is preferred because it is the sensor, and he explained its preeminence by the fact that the cerebral circuits on the right side are 200 times shorter than those on the left side. One can only wonder about the value of such reasoning, since it negates anatomical facts that have been known since Ambroise Paré.

In 1976, Tomatis resigned from the order of physicians (before the order had to render a ruling on his activity). But it was another 20 years before the Justice Department took an interest in the electronic ear.[5]

In 1988, a former patient of this guru of the golden ear, Mrs. Judith Many, rebelled. Suffering from Ménière's vertigo (a deterioration of the inner ear), she participated in 80 sessions of listening of Mozart at the Tomatis Center in Paris. Given the failure of these sessions, at full price, the Center offered her 80 additional meetings for free — with no greater success. Mrs. Many filed a complaint and, eight years later, Tomatis was fined $10,000 in amends.[6] The lawsuit charged that the "electronic ear" was only a cheap audiometer with no therapeutic function.

According to ear-nose-and-throat specialists, the Tomatis system is more like a religious pilgrimage to Lourdes than a scientific and therapeutic reality.

12. PSYCHIATRY AND DELUSIONS

Religion is the opium of the people.
Marx.

Therefore, render unto Caesar that which is Caesar's and to God that which is God's.
Matthew 22:21.

.

If there is any field where therapeutic delusions can be exercised without any limitation or possible control, it is that of psychiatry.

The field of physical suffering has certain characteristics that constrain the doctor and give patients some reference points by which they might judge the validity of the medical approach that is being offered. A bone fracture can be located and its progress in healing can be analyzed using X-rays. You can have an electrocardiogram to obtain comparative data, and you can take your temperature to see whether an anti-fever medication is working. In psychiatry, we have none of that. The doctor is constrained only by his own know-how and his personal ethics.

While we might envisage some form of tests to use in the case of definite, specific pathologies like psychosis or neurosis, there is no system by which one can check the validity of everyday psychiatric practices — neither in regard the diagnosis nor to the prescribed therapy. New means of research have been invented, like cerebral cartographies via technetium, but so far they are restricted to the domain of laboratory research — fortunately — and have not yet invaded the doctors' examination rooms.

Given that he has no tools, the patient has no frame of reference by which to differentiate between something that is an appropriate part of reasonable — albeit sometimes ineffective — practice, and something that is more in the domain of pickpockets, quacks, and delusionary pseudo-therapists. My 20 years of psychiatric practice have put me in contact with quite a number of patients who had been "treated" by crystal therapy, gemmo-therapy, vedic sophrology and foot massages.

In addition to the fact that we have no authentic system for charting the province of the mind, the field of psychiatric therapy is vulnerable to the recruitment of supposed therapists who find it a convenient discharge system for their own problems and fantasies.

Since time immemorial, mental therapy has been a field where science, magic and religion come together. In the Middle Ages, it was believed that epileptics were possessed by demons, and a certain religious influence can still be detected in that arena nowadays. Hysteria, with its great spectacular crises, was and still is the preferred area of activity for people who style themselves as exorcists, who consider the episodes a sign of the evil one's influence or even a manifestation of erotic relations with a succubus.

Many bridges have been built between psychiatry and certain religious or philosophical doctrines. In the 1960's, for example, psychiatrist-philosophizer Alan Watts made connections between Buddhism and psychiatry; at the same time, new movements were born that regard a certain religious or philosophical practice as a form of therapy. However, while these practices have a real didactic value and often represent a mode of expression and psychological progression, they should not be confused with therapeutic models; they cannot really handle the critical phases that "psychiatric sufferers" endure. Mastering a relaxation technique, meditation or visualization, certainly represents a positive step for an individual, but it is still necessary that the subject concerned should be in good enough shape to practice it coherently and that the practice not bring on additional more problems.

Cult groups and unscrupulous individuals frequently take advantage of the delirious or hallucinatory signs and symptoms of patients in a state of suffering. They claim the signs and symptoms are demonstrations of malevolent powers or evidence of the subject's past lives. I have noticed this on several occasions, when I have been called into various courts as expert witness to assess the psychiatric after-effects of such pseudo-medical practices.

A patient in need of psychological assistance or on a personal quest may thus place his fate in the hands of one of these many self-proclaimed healers, whose principle activity is selling a very personalized "therapy" derived from one or another psychiatric or psychoanalytical trend. The patient is also liable to fall into the hands of a more structured group that makes pompous claims of some psychoanalytical affiliation but in reality devotes itself to patently absurd practices.

The Paris School of Parapsychology

A case in point is the Paris School of Parapsychology, created in 1980 by Marguerite Preux. This school, which proclaims itself to be an initiatory group, promulgates a "whole life" teaching with the stated goal of leading the student to individualization. Madame Preux published a book in 1974 that seems to summarize her general view: *We Are All Animals.*

In 1977, she founded an association for psychic investigation, the purpose of which, in all modesty, was to study the phenomena concerned with psychophysiology, anthropology, metaphysics, parapsychology, human magnetism, human radiation, hypnotism, sophrology, psychoanalysis, suggestology, UFO's and mediums.

The program of the Paris School of Parapsychology is a hodgepodge of various borrowed sources grafted onto a trunk of patasciences both New Age and traditional — astrology, Tai-Chi-Chuan, Reiki — and also of traditional techniques of psychotherapy: psychodrama, psychoanalysis, music therapy. And for a touch of spice, since a hint of religion can do no harm to such an enterprise, Marguerite Preux invites her faithful flock of "immortals" to piously attend Mass during the high holy days. She recently asked her graduates to have their marriages blessed by the priest of Morsain, a remote town in the provinces (about as far as you can get from Paris, and still be in France), if possible in the City of Immortals — the unused train station.

The courses of the School of Parapsychology are spread out over three years, and during that time the followers must rebuild their lives according to new precepts enacted by Preux. This includes giving males and females a renewed sense of their respective duties in terms of the "traditional status of the sexes".

The Family of Nazareth

Another example is the Existential Psychoanalysis Workshop, also known as the Family of Nazareth. This group is the creation of Daniel Blanchard, who was trained in theology for a few years in Freiburg, after having been with the Benedictines of Solesmes, and after studying Jungian psychoanalysis for a few months. His psychoanalytical theory, as random as it is, brings in references and links between Reich's orgone, Janov's primal scream, and Jung's prototypes.

But Blanchard was not satisfied with teaching and applying the theories of his glorious elders, he came up with his own concepts, such as that of the "sub-ego" (a reference to Freud's "super-ego"), and nosographic entities such as the "schizonoïdia". His therapeutic practices are also rather curious: he goes from analytical relationship to therapeutic rest, then to psychodrama and group exercises. Blanchard's free-form psychoanalysis is paralleled by a structure inspired by the life of Jesus (which is why the group is named "Family of Nazareth"). This family is a community of lay people organized in five large groups, each of which is subdivided into three small families bearing the name of an apostle, a prophet or a saint.

Beside the (at the very least) weird character of this psychoanalytical/religious amalgam, one of the principle criticisms of this group is the quasi-dictatorial power that its founder has granted himself. In the group's statutes, it is explicitly stated that Daniel Blanchard is responsible for the unity of action and is vested with the powers necessary to that end, that he is the authority and is preeminent, and that he represents the common law.

The Institute of Psychoanalytical Research

Then we have the Institute of Psychoanalytical Research, which was created in 1978 by a psychologist, Maud Pison, trained in Freudian psychoanalysis. The IPR was in its glory until Pison and her right-hand man were convicted by the Draguignan correctional court.

After a beginning that could be described as traditional, Pison's psychoanalytical approach little by little strayed from the Freudian line and launched off into practices that were strongly marked by erotomaniac and megalomaniac delusions. Maud Pison, a reincarnation of the Virgin, officiated with the assistance of Dr. Galiano (a dental surgeon), her right-hand and a reincarnation of Jesus Christ. "Shock" psychoanalysis mixed together with Galiano's energy-odontological delusions; his preaching included the extraction of all lead-based fillings (liable to block the individual's energy flows), and allowing one's hair to grow freely (as receptors of these same energy flows). This practice, which really has to be qualified as paraphrenic, was put to rest in the court room, in 1997.

Besides the cult groups already mentioned, psychiatry and its related disciplines implicitly lead to the development of derivative groups that vary according to interpretation and theory. Seminars on sophrology or NLP (neurolinguistic programming) often serve as recruiting pools for organized groups.

Holistic psychiatry. Psychiatry is — by definition — a holistic discipline; it treats the person in his bodily, psychic and social entirety. A pathology like depression feeds on the most disparate sources, and a psychiatrist cannot skip over any branch of human activity. This essentially "holistic" approach did not, however, deter certain practitioners, who thought they had to invent the concept of holistic psychiatry from scratch. Thus we have associations such as the Negro Spiritual Emergency Network, the French Transpersonal Association and the International Association of Spiritual Psychiatry.

Conferences are held on various spiritual approaches to one or another pathology. While the intention of the participants is generally honest, there is every reason to fear that they are quickly overtaken by the missionaries of patamedicine, who are more concerned with recruitment than with any therapeutic effect. The position of Dr. C., a member of the *School of Transpersonal Energy*, illustrates very clearly the problems raised by spiritual psychiatry.

> Dr. C. subdivides life into two parts, each comprising four stages.
>
> The first of these stages is the schizoid, or autistic, position, with the problems of the fear of existing, the rejection of incarnation. . . . .
>
> The second stage is abandonism. The abandonic is one who, feeling abandoned, is filled with anger. . . .
>
> The third stage is self-centeredness, the need to bring back to oneself, to concentrate, the energies that are dispersed . . .
>
> The fourth stage is depression, in other words the result of the voyage in the external world. . . .
>
> In this spiritualistic view, depression is necessary since it marks the

end of the exploration of the external world, and the beginning of the "return trip".[1]

You can see that this interpretation of depression is a rehash of the concept of karma; the fatalistic aspect of the karmic doctrines incorporates the disease into a sterile form of resignation, if not a dynamic of guilt-tripping. The essential criticism that applies to these associations is that they approach psychosocial problems with a mystical dimension that inclines the person more to resignation than to any real dynamic of taking control. In an era when we see the management of social crises being transferred from the realm of politics to the realm of psychiatry, it is troubling to see psychiatric care being transferred to religion or religiosity.

For psychiatrists and psychotherapists who take a spiritual orientation, the human being has three traditional dimensions: the body, the soul and the spirit. Mental pathology is thus seen as having connotations of a spiritualistic dimension, so that it becomes possible to reintroduce concepts such as the soul, incarnation, karma, fear of the earthly — all concepts that belong to the religious domain and far from the fundamental diagnostic and therapeutic needs.

Ultimately, this approach is dangerous at a most profound level: it can take the place of analyzing the causes of phenomena like depression. Indeed, a state of depression that is a reaction to unemployment can easily be analyzed in terms of karmic life rather than in terms of economic crisis. Spiritual psychiatrists, by recommending meditation and prayer, in fact act as guardians of the established social order.

Spiritual psychiatry is thus reactionary, whereas real psychiatry aims to give the patient a capacity of individualization that, possibly, will enable him to question his status and the role that has been assigned to him in a system upon which he is dependent and which constrains him.

13. MEDICINE AND CULTS

Cults flourish in the field of health and disease, which gives them a context in which to expound their doctrines, as well as to conduct their research and to present evidence in support of the claims they make. The function of a cult is to lead the follower toward a model of personal fulfillment that fits in with the general theme of the group. Cults use disease as a proof of some form of deviance, of error, or even as the price of errors made in a former life. Through their doctrines and the resulting practices, the group tries to return the follower to the state of equilibrium that he is supposed to have lost. The teachings are thus reinforced by the individual's healing; the healing becomes proof of the doctrines' validity.

Medical concerns are the main focus of some groups' doctrines (instinct-therapy, Zen macrobiotics). Others derive some medical techniques from their general theories and teach them to all the followers or to a particular group (such as drug addicts). And others (Scientology, Grail) develop elaborate doctrines that arise from the leader's "medical" vision. Some groups are satisfied with spelling out an all-encompassing theory on the nature of man and his place in the cosmos, without venturing into the arena of diagnosis and treatment; others, however, expound whole treatises of medicine, published in the context of the group or by auxiliary groups.

Ageac, a Case in Point

Ageac[1] promotes medical doctrines that amount to an extremely precise theoretical corpus, a veritable therapeutic guide and a codex that reflect the thought of Samaël Aun Weor, the group's guru. These writings reveal the dangers that such groups pose for the health of the members. The theories described below are excerpted from Weor's writings, and specifically from the *Treatise on Occult Medicine and Practical Magic, Endocrinology and Criminology* and *Practice with the Elementals of the Physical Body*, works that are distributed by Ageac.

The theories that underlie their medical doctrines might be summarized thus:

1. Man cannot be reduced to his physical body alone. In reality, he is the terrestrial expression of a cosmic energy that traverses various levels and gradually manifests through them in two forms: the etheric body and the astral body (a reference to theosophy).

2. Man has five centers: intellectual, emotional, motor, instinctive, sexual.

3. The sexual center decides how man evolves and, by controlling it, man can decide his fate: self-realization or downfall (a reference to tantric yoga[2]).

Each center of the machine must function with its own energy, but unfortunately, the other centers of the machine steal the sexual energy. When the intellectual, emotional, motor and instinctive centers function incorrectly, they steal the sexual energy, and then we have sexual abuse. Sexual abuse ends when we establish inside ourselves a permanent center of gravity.

Naturally, the sexual center is the physical point where sexual hydrogen H Sill2 is produced, in a marvelous synthesis of the food we eat, the air we breathe and the input of all our impressions. From the transcendental and gnostic point of view, the following activities can be detected in the sexual center:

- reproduction of mankind;

- transformation of the "genetic libido", or "sexual libido", i.e. "the metal heart of the sacred sperm";

- creation of the Being's higher existential bodies;

- elimination of psychological flaws, with the help of the lance of Eros effectively in the grip of Devi-Kundalini, our personal, individual divine mother.

The sexual center can incontrovertibly be used as an instrument of the Being's manifestation, as long as we are liberated from the various "psychic aggregates" or "ego-defects".

This center functions poorly as a result of the "undesirable elements" of lust, secret or open adultery, homosexuality, lesbianism, and in general any type of sexual psychopathy.

Similarly, when the infra-instinctive "egos" block its delicate mechanisms, they cause all kinds of perversions that cause it to degenerate.[3]

This discourse gradually drifts away from rationality. While the concepts of tantric yoga can be justified by references to traditional teaching, the appearance of "sexual hydrogen" comes as a surprise, not to mention the condemnation of homosexuality, for example.

4. The practice of tantric yoga and sexuality enables man to reach a higher state. This leads to the "arcane AZF", which represents a form of both care and healing.

> The great physiologist Brown-Séquard, quoted by Dr. Krumm-Heller, invented a system of healing that many people have qualified as immoral. The system mentioned by Krumm-Heller consists in exciting the sexual apparatus without actually spilling the semen. Then, the semen is cerebralized and the brain is semenized. The semen is as-

similated into the organism and the nervous system is nourished and profoundly strengthened. This system is no obstacle to the reproduction of the species. A spermatozoon can easily escape from the organism without any need to disburse the hundred million spermatozoa that are lost in a seminal ejaculation.

The Brown-Séquard system is known in Italy as *caretza*. This is the arcane AZF.[4]

The real doctor must thus be a follower of *caretza*. The reference to a recognized figure from traditional medicine is used to cloud the issues and to create the sense of an amalgam between Brown-Séquard (the recognized medical reference) and Krumm-Heller (a cult reference).

Ageac rewrites physiology and pathology, mixing together precise data (when it comes to anatomy, for example) with wild imaginings.

Samaël Aun Weor lends an air of probability to his remarks by strewing them with authentic elements. Moreover, he magnifies their importance by presenting himself as the holder of secrets that were communicated to him either by his initiators or through a long secret tradition. Thus he weaves in contributions that include the Egyptian (the god Thot), Aztec (Quetzalcoatl), Indian (the theory of chakras), spiritist (etheric body, astral body) and numerous references intended to waylay the listener by inundating him under a wave of disparate and hard-to-verify sources.

After all these theoretical components have been run through the blender, the message delivered — combining elements of reality, historical references, and personal delusion — is sufficiently complex to defy analysis. Thus, little by little, physiological reality is reinterpreted and becomes a sign of sorcery or proof of occult powers.

The liver is the largest gland in the organism. . . . Doctors call it the organ of five. Cabbalists know that five is the number of Geburah,

Rigor, the Law. Certain mystics say that we have a crucified Christ in the liver. There is no doubt that the liver is the seat of the appetites and the desires. From this perspective, it is not certainly wrong to affirm that we have a crucified Christ in the liver.

The liver has five admirable lobes, five groups of harmonic conduits, five marvelous blood canals and five fundamental functions. *This number five, on which the liver is based, reminds us of the Law, Nemesis, that influences all these actions born of desire and of everything wicked.*

On the bronze liver discovered in the ruins of Piacenza, in Italy, inscriptions are engraved representing the twelve signs of the zodiac. It is said that ancient astrologers foretold the future by examining the liver of an animal. *They looked at the liver and on the basis of what they observed, they gave their prophecies.*

The entire zodiac of man-the-microcosm has its own laws and signs engraved in the liver.[5]

Using interpretations like this, the conduct of the group's members can be influenced, and they can be led to accept rules of living that are based on an interpretation of their health. Thus, the concept of karma encourages a fatal and morbid acceptance of disease in cult followers. Disease becomes a necessary experience or punishment. Certain diseases are presented as incurable: they are supposed to be the karmic result of grave errors made in an earlier life.

Since disease is an expression of a fault or of one's destiny, medicine is of no use. Only prayer or subservience to the law of the Master can give access to healing, and as corollaries this comes with the loss of one's own identity and the practice of tantric yoga.

Buddha, Jesus, Moses and others suffered great bitterness to deliver humanity from the disastrous after-effects of the Kundartiguator organ. The holy commission made up of ineffable beings took upon their shoulders a terrible cosmic karma; this karma will be paid in the next Mahamvantara. Hearken unto me, Brother Gnostics: understand that it is only with the three factors of the revolution of the conscience that you can be done with the harmful consequences of the Kundartiguator organ. These three factors are: the death of psychological ego, the birth of the Being within us, and the sacrifice for humanity.

The Ego can die only after a rigorous creative comprehension. The Being is born within us thanks to Maïthuna (sexual magic). The sacrifice for humanity is charity and love properly understood.

The schools that teach the ejaculation of semen, even if they do it in a very mystical way, are, in reality, black, because with this practice the Kundartiguator organ develops.

The schools that teach the Lingam-Yoni connection without ejaculation of the semen are white, for thus Kundalini goes up into the medullary canal.

The schools that teach the strengthening of the psychological ego are black, for the disastrous consequences of the Kundartiguator organ are thus reinforced.

The schools that teach the dissolution of the ego (mystical death) are white, because the evil consequences of the Kundartiguator organ are then destroyed. The Kundartiguator organ is the tail of Satanas, sexual fire going down from the coccyx to the atomic hells of man.[6]

Ageac's way of treating non-karmic diseases is a reprise of ancient witches' brews that continue to be popular in various corners of society. Animal products, for example, are used to place the patient in a relationship with the magical power that is attributed to one or another animal. Thus the rhinoceros and the elephants are decimated: people try to adapt the supposed phallic and generative powers contained in their horns and their defensive structures; the same applies to the Bengal tiger, whose penis, dried and powdered, is supposed to encourage the procreation of male heirs.

Wizards' spells abound with recipes where slime of toad mixes with lizard's skin, batwings and cobwebs. The "gnostics" of Ageac are great fans of these "remedies" and update them with a breath of youth that places them halfway between old wives' tales and witches' potions.

> Applying the rattles of the rattlesnake, dissected and wrapped in gauze, to the ears, will make deafness and earaches go away.

> Placing a rattle on hot coals, in a vessel, and sitting in such a way as to inhale the vapors, cures disturbances of the uterus; the patient must keep away from the cold and even from drafts.

> Skunk liver, pulverized and taken in a cup of hot water, is an effective sudorific and is good for spasms, chest problems, colds, fevers and for diseases of the respiratory tract in general.

> We have heard that the flesh of the skunk is good for curing syphilis; you have to keep eating it until your health is restored.

Sometimes taking an animal potion is not enough, and one must have recourse to more "traditional" remedies — alcohol, tobacco, etc. — without giving up the magic side. In that case, the one who is administering the remedy may talk about the cause of the disease.

> The decoction of the plant called "wormwood" [absinthe], taken on an empty stomach several mornings in a row, evacuates worms from the belly and even tapeworm. In this ultimate case, speaking of the terrible tapeworm, you take the juice of wormwood, two or three small spoonfuls, mixed with powdered mint.

If this peasant magic is not enough, more radical solutions will be considered: the occult powers will be called in, using the entire arsenal of traditional magic.

> Tobacco is used against epilepsy in the following way. Take one ounce of good quality tobacco, shredded into small pieces; place it in a pot or a container with a bottle of water and place it on the stove to boil. After it has boiled sufficiently, remove it from the heat; allow it to cool, and add three ounces of sugar to it; return the pot to the stove and boil until the decoction becomes syrupy. Take two spoonfuls morning and evening, while drinking a medium-sized glass of decoction of elder flowers, in addition. Stay in bed for at least three hours after each dose.

> In addition, the patient must recite with great faith conjuration VII of Solomon the Wise.

> The magic symbol of the esoteric pentagram should be hung above the epilepsy patient's head, on headboard of the bed; it drives away demons.

> Epilepsy is due to the karma of the patient who, in lives past, served as a medium for contact with spirits.

> Epileptics should never visit spiritism parlors or participate in *séances*.

Ageac derives its information from many sources — authentic symbolism, occult or esoteric references, and Samaël Aun Weor's personal delusions — and the mixture leads the listener to feel that the spiel is credible since it draws on recognized or supposedly recognized concepts (like Hippocrates, or Viracocha, who become Harpocrates and Huiracocha in the following example).

> Thus, logic invites us to think that great occult powers exist in the egg. Guru Litelantes explained to me the magic formula of the egg.

Guru Litelantes said to me that with an egg, a person could place his physical body in a genie state. You have to make a small hole in the pointed end of the egg and blow the yoke and egg white through this hole. Warm the egg a little, in water, before making the hole. The disciple will then paint the eggshell blue. Place the shell near the bed, and the disciple will fall asleep thinking of himself curled up inside the eggshell.

Master Huiracocha says that in these moments, one must call upon the god Harpocrates while pronouncing the following mantra: HAR-PO-CRAT-IST. Then the god Harpocrates will introduce the disciple into the egg. The disciple will feel a great itching or tingling on his body.

In the beginning, the student may succeed in transporting himself in his astral body. Later, the student will be able to move with his physical body in a genie state. That takes a great deal of practice and tenacity.

The genie state allows us to work all these wonders. Guru Litelantes showed me how a physical body in a genie state can assume various forms and increase and reduce its size at will.

Really, official medicine does not know the physical body except in its purely primary or elementary aspects. Scientists are completely unaware that the physical body is plastic and elastic. Official studies of anatomy and physiology are still in an embryonic state.

The forces that Guru Litelantes taught me to manage are the Harpocratian forces that are palpitating and coursing through the entire universe.

The HAR-PO-CRAT-IST forces are an alternative to the Christic forces.

One really has to wonder about the psychic equilibrium of group members who run after rattlesnakes and skunks, who seek to talk face-to-face with their tapeworms and who travel in an eggshell.

Healing Cults on the Rise

Some of the healing cults have expanded in recent years.

Mahikari

Carried along on the wave of Buddhist movements in the 1970s and 1980s, Sukyô Mahikari (Light of Truth) is a cult that was founded in 1969 in Japan by Kôtama Okada, a one-time arms dealer and an officer in the Japanese imperial guard who was brought to financial ruin by the destruction of his weapons factories.[7]

After having received a revelation from the god Sû (Sumokami = creative God, supreme God) "on February 22, 1959, early in the morning", the founder faithfully went forth to fulfill his mission of "being a sphere of light".

In 1969, he published *Goseigen*, a book of holy words, which became the cult's bible. Upon Okada's death in 1974, his disciples (who seem not to have mastered their guru's precepts of wisdom), fell into conflict and his successors, whose interests were complicated by financial considerations, had to call in the Japanese court system to distribute the guru's holy heritage. The principal branch devolved to Sekigutchi, testamentary successor of Okada, while a minority branch went with Keiju Okada, daughter of the founder. In France, it is the second branch that controls most of the associations known as the Light of Truth.

After having received the 22 revelations from the god Sû, Okada, who in all modesty positioned himself in the lineage of Moses, Çakyamuni, Jesus and Mohammed, proclaimed the Mahikari sacred principles of healing. Obviously influenced by the bombings of Hiroshima and Nagasaki and by the mercury pollution of Minimata, Okada proclaimed that spiritual impurities are the cause of all our planetary evils — including not only pollution but medicine and medical intoxication.

The Mahikari art of healing consists in transmitting the divine light via the palm of the hand, an operation known as Okiyome. This operation makes it possible to cure the gravest pathologies and to eliminate all toxins. The miraculous healing is one of the traditional implements of Mahikari and strangely enough recalls the words of Christ. The Mahikari command, "Rise, speak your name and raise your hand" replaces the "Rise and go forth" of the Gospels.

> What help does our movement, Seikai Mahikari Bunmei Kyodan, offer, and how can it achieve miracles?

> In dojos throughout the whole world, the leaders and all the initiates as well can practice the art of Mahikari by raising their hands. These initiates, who bear the name of Kami Kumités or Yokoshis, can bring the spiritual assistance necessary to the resolution of health problems; everyday illnesses, wounds, or diseases often considered to be incurable — cancer, heart problems, liver, kidneys, brain, and stomach trouble, and psychiatric problems. Better yet, they can help to solve all kinds of difficulties: family and other conflicts, professional difficulties. 90% of the people who turn to these initiates see their problems resolved.[8]

The propositions espoused in Mahikari are peppered with traditional references to medical esotericism — for example, concerning the role of the pineal gland.

> When one raises the hand to practice the art of Mahikari and to transmit the light of the truth to the pineal gland, where the soul is located, behind the face, the spirits that are possessing the individual start to appear, in suffering. The face of the person possessed is

transformed into that of the possessing spirit, or his hands, which are clasped, start to move. There may be manifestations that indicate how the possessing spirit lived before death, or how he died. The manifestations are all very different, one from another.[9]

This power is not reserved to advanced initiates alone, but can accrue to any follower provided that he adheres to Mahikari and receives the holy talisman: Omitama.

> When you receive purification through practicing the art of Mahikari, you will notice yourself that this purification brings something new to you. You will be astonished to have miraculous experiences, such as you never experienced before.

> During this initiation, you will receive lessons on the principles of the universe that are completely different from all that you learned hitherto. You will feel spiritually awakened.

> Anybody, no matter who, man or woman, regardless of his religion, his age, can become an initiate.

> At the end of the course, you will be given Omitama, a spiritual medallion, which will ensure your spiritual bond with God, and immediately afterwards, you will be able to learn how one must practice the art of Mahikari and the giving of Light.

> Thus you will become a man who can perform miracles. The miracles will be renewed each time you raise your hand.

> You will free yourselves from your problems, you will help others to solve their problems, all thanks to the Light of God. You will be astonished by the miracles that are thus performed. You will know a happy life and will have Ken, Wa, and Fu, the three conditions of happiness.[10]

Mahikari rejects all contemporary medical practice, since modern medicine is regarded as unable to treat any pathology and as being responsible for poisoning the patients. Followers must have faith only in the healing power of Mahikari.

> Incurable disease does not exist, except in exceptional cases where God does not forgive.

On the contrary, traditional care is condemned outright.

> Therapies make people believe they have been cured. But they result in the accumulation of the following serious problems: stagnation of toxins, repeated intoxication, destruction of the human body through surgery.[11]

The danger of Mahikari lies in the fact that the cult does not stop at preaching miracle cures, but spreads untruths that are likely to cause medical accidents.

> Fever plays a very important part in divine work, due to the love of God, so that humanity can know the state in which it will not be subjected to disease anymore. Benefiting from fever is the first step for men to be able to live as long as God envisaged.

> It's bad to brush your teeth; the effect of tooth-brushing in preventing dental decay is very doubtful.[12]

This opposition to traditional medicine does not prevent Mahikari from recruiting followers in the medical field and from using doctors as its recruiting sergeants, in particular in the field of psychiatry, where the patients seem to be easier to manipulate because of their existential questions and their fragility.

Invitation to Intense Life (IVI)

This cult frequently has been in the forensic news, in the last sev-eral years.[13] It was founded by the French-woman Yvonne Trubert. Persuaded that she has the power of healing, she frequented healers and hypnotists, familiarized herself with esoteric and occultist literature, and began to counsel and care for numerous people. Her reputation grew, in particular in middle-class Catholic circles, when she claimed that her "healings" occur only through prayer. Since 1980, with some of the families that have enjoyed her care, she has organized and led prayer and healing groups.

The doctrine of the cult is summarized as "Pray, Love, Cure"; and the divine mission that Yvonne Trubert says she is pursuing is "to re-veal a new religion, a new world and a new medicine". The religious teaching that she dispenses is an odd blend of Christianity, Hinduism and esoteric theories. The members of IVI are the reincarnation of the five thousand disciples who followed Christ. The twelve principal leaders of IVI are the reincarnation of the twelve apostles. Trubert is a reincarnation of Christ, the Virgin Mary or the Holy Spirit, according to the needs of the moment. The demon is present and within all, eve-rywhere, and IVI members receive the power to drive out and exorcize these demons.

Trubert teaches that she cures all diseases: leukemia, lymphoma, bone cancer, lung cancer, and even AIDS. "There is no incurable dis-ease." This medical teaching is spelled out in a book entitled: *New Man, New Medicine*, a document "for internal use", which can be distributed only to IVI members who have participated in an initiatory seminar. Since its creation, IVI "medical research" has made great progress thanks to its Private Hospital, where members of IVI who belong to medical or ancillary medical professions and the more abtruse disci-plines (astrology, holo-therapy, chrono-therapy. . .) meet every month.

IVI has discovered "Marian, metal and water medicine":

> We work on metals, whose vibrating electronic layers hold the memories of our families and our lives, and we work on water, which lovingly records, the better to entrust it to she who contains it: Mary.

> While working on metals and water, we touch ADN: the photons that metals release, via water, strike and regenerate this ADN. In the ADN is contained the essence: ADN = HEART. Recognition of the intercellular metallic capital is achieved by analyzing the hair by atomic spectroscopy, for our hair is our antenna.

> IVI has opened treatment centers where "harmonizations" and "vibrations" are practiced. Trubert and her followers say that harmonization consists in restoring the harmony between the three bodies (physical, energy and astral) while freeing the chakras via actions that can be taken at a distance from the patient's body.

Vibrations, the third method recommended by IVI, are presented as cosmic jolts that enable the individual to jump to another vibratory frequency and thus to escape terrestrial laws. These vibrations are obtained through group recitation of mantras that should propel the followers to unknown worlds that have been lost for millennia. "At IVI, we vibrate in a group, we vibrate at home and in triad, on pilgrimage, and nowadays even harmonization beds are equipped with a vibratory system." The "song of the heart" is a very new discovery: "the vibratory song gives access to the total reactivation and realization of our being."

Trubert says that her work is divine work, and "nothing will keep [her] from achieving it". "As for the organizational structure of IVI, if Christ returned in the current century, he would have to create an organization like *Invitation to Life*. He could not do otherwise." While waiting to be identified as the new Messiah, Yvonne Trubert teaches her disciples that "what medicine calls 'incurable, never believe it: there are no incurable diseases. . . . All you have to do is pray, and the miracle is performed. . . . Metastases will fly away under your fingers. You needn't trouble yourself as to how. What I want to say to you is that they will disappear. . ."

The disintegration of metastases has not always been successful. Following IVI's practices, as we will see below, has caused at least one disciple (who was a doctor) to be barred from practicing medicine, for the rest of his life.

The World Happiness Organization

Periodically, the world of medicine is virulently assaulted by some enlightened being who is convinced he has discovered the medical Fountain of Youth, and who is also convinced that, because of his discovery, he has become the target of the great pharmaceutical companies, the CIA, the medical mafia or, better yet, of a global political-economic plot.

The latest of these enlightened spirits is a woman who recently settled in France after having been convicted of criminal activity in Quebec, where she began her career. From 1984 to 1990, Dr. Ghislaine Lanctôt exercised her art in Florida, where she treated varicose veins.

At the end of 1994, she signed her name to a work that became a bestseller in the world of "anti-medical ranting and raving", entitled *The Medical Mafia*. In this work, Dr. Lanctôt denounces all the advances that have been made in medicine, expounding her own doctrines based on the rejection of proven techniques — first and foremost, the vaccination and health care programs provided by the World Health Organization and the National Institute of Health.

Like any good paranoiac guru, Lanctôt sees enemies everywhere and her discourse borrows many themes from neo-Nazi rightwing extremists. Denying the evidence of our planet's medical evolution, she proclaims such nonsensical beliefs that any impartial observer should easily reject — which, unfortunately, is not the case of the members of the World Happiness Organization, a group that she has been striving to establish in Europe since 1995.

> The medical authorities teach us that vaccines protect us from viruses and germs that may attack the organism, and thus they prevent contagious diseases and epidemics.
>
> This enormous lie has remained in place for 150 years, in spite of the vaccines' inability to protect us from diseases. . . .
>
> The uselessness of certain vaccines [is obvious], especially for diseases such as:
>
> • Tuberculosis and Tetanus. These vaccines never confer immunity. The fact of having had tuberculosis does not prevent us from getting it again. On the contrary, the first attack of tuberculosis (sometimes caused by the vaccine) leaves the person far more vulnerable to a second episode, which is often fatal;
>
> • Rubella, against which 90% of the women of any population are naturally protected anyway. The risks associated with the disease are limited to the first three months of pregnancy; however, they vaccinate the entire population, including boys.
>
> • Diphtheria. Even at the height of the greatest epidemics, only 7% of the children were infected. However, they are all vaccinated. And what is more, children and adults are repeatedly vaccinated, although it is claimed that only a vaccine received during childhood ensures immunity *ad vitam aeternam.*
>
> • Influenza and Hepatitis B, whose viruses quickly become strongly resistant to the vaccines' antibodies. These two vaccines are then completely useless, and in addition they are extremely dangerous.
>
> The best source of immunity is natural immunity. And that is normally found in 80% to 90% of the population before the age of fifteen years. Because all the organism's defense systems are mobilized when a person is contaminated by a disease, natural immunization occurs

in an orderly way. On the contrary, contamination via vaccine short-circuits all the first lines of defense. Artificial immunization takes place in disorder. So it is not surprising that it requires frequent repetition... as futile as the vaccines themselves![14]

Just reading these assertions, you can see that they are spurious. Everyone knows that tuberculosis has been practically eradicated, thanks to vaccination, and that it is the faulty application of the vaccination process, coupled with the extreme poverty in some parts of the world, that cause its recrudescence. Anti-rubeola vaccination is not systematically offered to boys, for this is a relatively benign disease; the only real danger that rubella presents is the risk of causing deformities in unborn children. All the vaccination programs against diphtheria require repetition, contrary to Lanctôt's assertion. Hepatitis B has been controlled perfectly by vaccination. As for influenza, if vaccination is not 100% effective, that is because the virus is constantly mutating, and not because the vaccines don't work.

The dichotomy that Lanctôt evokes between natural immunization and artificial immunization is also highly suspect. Vaccination means stimulating the organism's immunity by a natural reaction, which produces antibodies in response to an antigen that has been introduced in a weakened form, derived from natural organisms. Only the process by which it is administered is "artificial", which does not sully in any way the "naturalness" of the immunizing phenomenon.

Lanctôt takes full advantage of the anti-vaccination prejudice held by some parts of the population, by weaving together her own personal interpretations, contemporary medical problems, and a very skewed global political vision. She does not recoil from propagating the nuttiest rumors, and her platform includes signs of her rightwing inspiration. She denounces the "new world order", a "plot by the multinational corporations", the "loss of family identity" and the "monitoring of citizens".

During her trial before the Quebec College of Doctors, in August

1995, she did not take too much trouble over the details: she claimed that vaccinations were the cause of cancer, of AIDS, and also led to children being born with mouse tails and rabbit fur. She inspired the wrath of her fellow-members, and in particular of Dr. Chicoine, a pediatric doctor and assistant professor at the University of Montreal, who had studied her writings carefully. "In a text of more than sixty pages, Dr. Chicoine denounces 'the home-grown delusions that Mrs. Lanctôt imposes with impunity on public health'.[15]"

In summary, the doctor reproaches her for having focused attention only on the potential side-effects of the vaccines, while carefully avoiding any discussion of their advantages, which far outweigh their disadvantages. During the trial, Dr. Chicoine announced that, with contagious diseases, there are probably 1000 – 5000 times more serious complications in people who have not been vaccinated than in those who have been protected by a vaccine. And he added:

> Mrs. Lanctôt indulges in "scientific pornography", based on "revelations" and alleged "research", in order to sow fear. There are no analyses, no references, no statistics, and no methodology for Ghislaine Lanctôt.

However, the doctor does not underestimate the threatening and anxiety-inducing power of Mrs. Lanctôt's theories, for he could not fail to see it in the course of his work. "Rarely have so many intelligent and judicious moms and dads asked so many stupid, idiotic questions; that is what fear does".

The 1995 trial underscored Ghislaine Lanctôt's inspirations.

> A thorough analysis of the reading list Lanctôt recommends to readers in her book, *The Medical Mafia*, shows that her bibliographical sources include a multitude of authors known to be American, French and Canadian far right militants.

Several works by Henry Coston, a notorious French anti-Semite, [are mentioned]; he is one of those who denounce the "Judeo-Masonic plot", and he was in contact with the Nazi propaganda services during the Second World War, [along with] the books by Toronto professor Robert O'Driscoll, who maintains (among other things) that the Jews are conspiring with the freemasons to found the "world reign of the Antichrist".[16]

Questioned as to these bibliographical sources, during the hearings before the College of Doctors, Mrs. Lanctôt played down the importance of the ideological affiliation of the authors whom she quotes, and declared that she herself was "convinced that it is in the public's interest to be aware of these works".

IHUERI

The spiritual school of universal energy may not have been the first to propagate the ideas of universal energy and the theory of chakras, but it seems to be one of the precursors of the popularization of these theories in the Western world, and was among the first to adapt them to the medical context.

IHUERI (The International Human and Universal Energy Research Institute) was founded early in the 20th century by a Sri Lankan, Dasira Narada. Following a career as a high civil servant, this doctor of philosophy began teaching the precepts of what would become IHUERI. In 1906, he withdrew from the material world to contemplate and to pursue his own spiritual life.

His successor, Narada II, followed the traditional disciple-master relationship; he taught until in 1972, when he transmitted his knowledge and the leadership role in IHUERI to a Vietnamese by the name of Lvong Minh Dang, who took the title of Narada III. His disciples call him Master Dang. Taking advantage of the Western passion for Far-Eastern philosophies and spiritual movements, IHUERI gradually es-

tablished itself in the United States, then in Europe. A group was created in France in 1991.

According to Master Dang, the teaching of universal energy has
several objectives, including personal growth, alternative medicine and
humanitarian aid. This teaching is presented in three stages. First, the
follower must learn how to open his chakras to overcome universal energy and to maintain good health; then he must also look after others,
treating both minor illnesses and incurable diseases; finally, he must
develop his love for suffering humanity, in order to evolve spiritually.

According to the adherents of IHUERI, the first three levels of the
teaching are centered on patient care. The three subsequent levels,
which are given only in St. Louis, Missouri, are exclusively devoted to
spirituality; the seventh degree trains disciples chosen by the Master to
assist him and succeed to him.

> The program offered to members for acquiring mastery over the
> "universal and human" energy is articulated in five or six chapters and
> as many training courses, each recognized with an in-house di-
> ploma. . . .

> "At Level I, one can only treat simple diseases. . .", explains the notice
> given to the trainees.

> At Level II, with a greater "opening of the chakras" (60%), the mem-
> bers can take care of up to twenty people per day. . . .

> At Level III, the pivotal point in the training, the approach becomes
> more coercive. During these sessions, the "master" displaces himself
> in flesh and in chakras. "Authoritative and threatening", according to
> one trainee. . . . At this stage, the student benefits from a 100% open-
> ing of his chakras and can thus provide care for all diseases.

> The second part of Level III, which is pursued by fewer aspirants,
> opens up an unvarnished esoterical discourse. There is no formal

prohibition against discussing the curriculum, but the warning is firm: "You will not be understood, people will think you are mad". "The mental manipulation is insidious", sighs Hortense [a former member].[17]

It is hardly surprising to discover, while reading the group's "internal documents," that "to open your chakras" you have to recognize Dang as master, and that disavowing him would mean the closing of one's chakras.

The heritage proclaimed by Master Dang certainly authorizes the master to demand respect in every instance, since he is nothing less than the reincarnation the Empress Gia Long, sent to earth to complete the work of Buddha and of Jesus.[18]

In fact, if IHUERI and its offshoots were satisfied just to teach spirituality and techniques of personal growth, no one would find any reason to object. What is more problematic is that Master Dang and his disciples target their recruitment on the medical field, and they claim that harmonization and the opening of the chakras cure all disease, from the simplest to the most serious:

Here is Master Dang's "decree" of January 30, 1996:

Master Dang authorizes to treat the AIDS and addiction:

1) All Centers of Universal Energy in every country;
2) All holders of Level 5;
3) All the trainees who have attended the special session on treating diseases by Chakra 6 (trainees who have attained Level 3 or Level 4 are authorized to treat AIDS and addiction only within their family);
4) All doctors, including those who do not work in the centers, even if they have only attained Level 3 or Level 4;
5) All trainees who are not part of a center's staff must, after having treated AIDS and addiction, inform the nearest center. All the Centers in every country will inform the Research Institute in St. Louis, who will report to Master Luong Minh Dang on the matter.

6) This decree takes effect as of 01/30/96.

Despite having been nailed by the parliamentary report on cults, IHUERI has in no way lessened its proselytizing through all its related associations: IREHU, CREHU, HUE, Energy, Universal and Human Energy, Energy and Sharing, SEVA, CRYSTAL, and through associations set up to "assist" victims of AIDS (Sidamour) and those who are dying.[19]

In the great tradition of cults that want to achieve social recognition, the followers of IHUERI collaborate with organizations such as WHO in providing humanitarian aid to developing countries — a technique that enables them to proselytize in areas where a piece of bread can buy a conversion. Now, IHUERI is planning to open treatment centers in Southeast Asia.

Energo-Chromo-Kinesis

Energo-Chromo-Kinesis, or ECK, is one of the most powerful cults in the medical world, where it recruits doctors, physical therapists, nurses and dental surgeons. Created by Patrick Véret in 1987, it has taken advantage of the confusion that arises from the fact that Véret was a member of the National Order of Physicians and was a practicing doctor until recently. Nearly 400 doctors thus became disciples of Véret and have declared themselves energeticians.[20] Its creators say that:

> Energo-Chromo-Kinesis brings everyone the tangible reality of his existence. It reveals the genetic programming that, like a program, makes us act consciously or unconsciously. Thanks to this genetic program, decoded by scientific techniques, the fruit of rigorous and objective research, each participant can find the very essence of his existence and of his overall destiny.

Energo-Chromo-Kinesis makes it possible to activate the energies that animate us. Learning how to master them by using sound and color enables us to attain our maximum potential in a short time. These workshops are based on neither the intellect nor on mental exercise. They are unique in that they work through vibratory experience and sensation that make it possible to be in harmony with oneself and one's environment.

ECK's doctrines are particularly persuasive in that they represent an amalgam (or a synthesis, according to its proponents) of various theories referring to human "energy" — mainly Chinese medicine and Vedic medicine.

According to ECK, the human body has seven energy centers that vibrate on the same frequencies as certain colors and certain sounds. Each of these centers corresponds to certain psychological qualities: joy, anger, lust, cynicism. Diagnosis thus consists in establishing, first of all, the subject's frequential or harmonic type, which can be represented by just one color on a spectrum with seven nuances.

Patrick Véret considers that the energetician-doctor must be capable of "true vibratory sensation".

The cosmogonic man must perceive the quality of the vibrations emitted by human organisms; the vibrations are of different frequencies, different wavelengths (thus different colors) depending on what part of the body is considered. This is an idea that is also found in ayurvedic medicine. The genital area normally would vibrate in red, the belly in orange, the solar plexus in yellow, the heart in green, the throat in purple, the brain in blue, and above the head, one should "perceive" indigo. Man is like a great natural kaleiodoscope, and disease, discomfort, would be translated by an ECK kinergist, as "a color that doesn't go well, or that vibrates in the wrong place".[21]

When the subject is vibrating on the nuance that suits him, his pulse is stronger; otherwise, it declines. The kinergist, who uses references to the Chinese pulse, assigns a mark from 1 to 7 on a diagram, which becomes the subject's energy morpho-psychogram. The ECK energetician-therapist's job is thus to diagnose the flow of colors, to deduce from it any organic attacks or functional disorders, to propose appropriate treatments and to verify their effectiveness by seeing that the vibrations have returned to normal.

To conduct the initial diagnosis, the expert takes with the patient's pulse with one hand, while passing a quartz prism over him with the other hand (no need to disrobe). The quartz enters into resonance with the patient's vibrations that are felt via the pulse. ECK energeticians believe that the pulse is slower if there is disharmony (and therefore a problem) at the place above which the prism is held, or on the contrary the pulse is stronger if all is well. In addition, taking the pulse is an essential part of the ECK energetician's way of deciding on a prescription. For this, the patient holds a glass tube in his hand, with the proposed drug (homeopathic, antibiotic, or what have you). The expert notes the level of the pulse to see whether or not there is resonance.

Patrick Véret also uses two tests, very spectacular when they are carried out by a group. The first test relates to three points — called ionic — located on the inner side of the foot, above the knee, and on the sternum. These points appear to be particularly sensitive to the expert's touch (to the point of eliciting cries of pain!) when the patient holds in his hand a substance or a color that is not appropriate to him.

The second test, "muscular testing" (on which Véret has no monopoly), consists in testing the individual's muscular resistance, a resistance that decreases considerably when he is holding on him an element that disturbs his electromagnetic field.[22]

Each center is tested twice, first using a yin energy source, the second time with yang. This leads to the establishment of a diagram with two curves is: the first represents the person's current experience, the second depicts his energy potential. If the two curves overlap, that means that the pupil has utilized his energy capacities as well as possible; if they diverge, that means that the energy is out of balance. This can be cured through kinergetics sessions. In this view, food is considered an optimal solution: all you have to do is get nutri-food marketed by Cogego Laboratory, where Véret works as supervising doctor.[23] ECK members and energetician-doctors regularly consume nutriments from organ meat, nutri-yin, nutri-yang, metals and amino acids that are supposed to restore their defective energy balances and to reunite them with the great primordial energy source.

These products were studied at the behest of the national pharmacists' organization. The verdict is clear:

> These are not medications. This is charlatanism. These products do not offer any protection, they contain extremely low amounts of nutrients, the packaging provides no therapeutic indications, no instructions, and no true formula.[24]

The founder of ECK says, on the contrary, that eating nutri-food "allows the subject to elevate his vibratory level via his consciousness, through a practical and objective approach to the constant relationships between energy and the presentation of pathological symptoms". In his book, *Introduction to Energy-Medicine*, one can read:

> There is an energy-based way to approach the incidence of diabetes. It would be interesting to see which energy disorders might, at low vibrations, have induced this biological modification. Most of the time. . . , patients are regarded as functional or as psychic units. In fact, it is a manifestation that corresponds to energy disorders that went untreated.

It is hard to fight such absurdities when the promulgation of Chinese energy theories and homeo-energetic raving is accepted by the general public.

ECK has managed to cobble together a set of doctrines based on disparate elements from homeopathy spiced up with Tao (sprinkled with a bit of yin and yang), chromotherapy (the use of colors), biofeedback and acupuncture. By using the traditional links of patamedicine, ECK was able to carve out its medical niche quickly and thus was able to recruit members in the medical and medical services milieu.

In a 1992 study addressed to the [French] Association for the Defense of Families and the Individual, the Health Ministry expressed the opinion of the National Academy of Medicine:

> Energo-medicine has no scientific basis. It rests on assertions, not reasoning. It is justified by no quantified data of a clinical, therapeutic or statistical nature. Its teaching cannot be authorized and its practical exercise does not appear to be compatible with the elementary principles of medical-professional deontology.

However, ECK's founders do not stop at reinterpreting traditional energy medicine. They have far more esoteric goals — in the worst sense of the term. ECK is not only an association with medical and ancillary medical goals, it has created a structure where secrecy is the rule of operation. Admittedly, one might say that they need to keep their light under the bushel — so that it does not blind everyone — but in medical matters, since the Inquisition, medical works have been available to all, with unrestricted access, and that is not the rule with ECK's lessons:

> To you, student of the Energo-chromo-kinesis school, . . . This book will enable you to continue working on yourself, and that is why you have been given your own copy at the end of the session.

> The teaching can be transmitted only by kinergists who have been trained, and who have the right vibratory level to do it. It is thus impossible and even dangerous to try to pass on that which has been transmitted to you.

Energo-chromo-kinesis has enabled you to find or to strengthen your own identity by rebalancing your diagram . . . You, holder of this book, can show your respect for the other by not divulging the contents. May this book be the vector of new awareness.[25]

Thus begins the foreword of the 1988 edition of *Energo-chromo-kinesis*, a work by Patrick Véret and Danielle Dronant. The suggested program is mighty skimpy when it comes to medicine and is heavily connoted with New Age mysticism:

> We will teach you how to balance your physical body while augmenting your telluric energies through your seven energy centers, with the assistance of colors and sounds. . . .

> You will learn how to feel these energies on a vibratory level. Thus, you will become "operative". You will learn how to use these energies as a practitioner of energy transfers on plants.

> You will be able to use your subtle bodies, knowing how to put yourself in your "driver's seat", your etheric brain.

These doctrines make it clear that ECK is part of that great wave of movements that are on a quest for the divine, and they are the basis for the movement's internal structure as it applies to the elite (Stage 3 of the members). After a testing period of several months and close "supervision", the candidate is allowed into the "The New Order of Operative Templars" — provided his energy level is high enough. At this stage, ECK reveals itself as what it really is: a recruiting ground for the creation of a pseudo-chivalric and elitist order whose bases are roughly outlined in the *Introduction to Energo-Medicine*.

> 20th century man is confronted with the problem of pollution at every level.

Pollution of his environment: The seas are dying because of all waste that is being dumped there. Countries are fighting not to be on the receiving end of all this waste from toxic industries.

Pollution of himself, from taking tranquilizers to enable himself to go on living, without coming to the necessary realizations and awakenings. He thus lives as a permanent zombie, on these pills of happiness, expecting a material improvement in his existence — the point of which he no longer understands.

This pollution is also that of men compared to other men, who seek to impose their own ideology by making war.

(Véret's discourse shows strange analogies with that of Luc Jouret.)

The Earth is tightly connected with the planets of this solar system and is subject to the laws that allow this connection of the elements each to the others and the constant recognition that makes it possible for this system to exist. . . .

There is a total interdependence between the whole and the man and the man and the whole. The whole is in the whole. The microcosm is made in the image of the macrocosm. From the infinitely small to the infinitely large, the same unity of creation is found.

Energy medicine makes it possible to integrate man and his environment and to give him back his real dimension in his affiliation to creation. Thus will one be able to apprehend pathology, no longer as a fate but indeed as the language of the physical body. Pain, the expression of the energy of suffering, will enable the being to become aware of his errors of operation in regard to the existential laws of creation.

The Hamer Method

The Hamer method is not quite an organized cult group, but it is the inspiration behind several medical and ancillary medical movements that are gaining ground in Germany, Switzerland, Belgium and France.

Dr. Hamer's story reads like the invented autobiographies of a guru, but it has been authenticated by the press. Director of Internal Medicine at an academic hospital in Cologne, after having been a practicing physician in Heidelberg from 1967 to 1976, Dr. Geerd Ryke Hamer had his life torn apart in 1978 when his son Dirk, on vacation in Corsica, was fatally wounded by a projectile that was fired during a brawl on a nearby yacht (on which Prince Victor-Emmanuel of Savoy was a passenger, among others). The death of his son and the prince's conviction for the relatively minor charge of weapons possession afflicted Dr. Hamer deeply. A few months later, he was diagnosed with cancer; it was treated and cured by traditional techniques.

Marked by this series of painful experiences, Hamer then plunged into total insanity, which led him to develop what he would later call the "bronze law of cancer":

> Cancer always begins with an extremely brutal shock, an acute and dramatic conflict, experienced in isolation and perceived by the patient as the most serious that he has ever felt.[26]

He wrote up this theory in a report that gives it the name of the *Dirk Hamer Syndrome* — named for his dead son. The Dirk Hamer syndrome is the subjective perception of a conflict that supposedly causes a "Hamer hotspot, i.e. a rupture of the field in a specific area of the brain that then gives anarchistic directives to the cells of the organ linked to that region". This leads to the conclusion that "there is an exact correlation between how the conflict evolves and the cancer at both the cerebral and organic level."[27] Hamer uses the "bronze law" to explain all physical and mental pathology, and above all what we call serious diseases such as AIDS, cancer and multiple sclerosis.

In Hamer's eyes, all external interventions like "traditional" treatments are new aggressions and new shocks that, due to "mental integration", induce new pathologies or accelerate the development of existing pathologies. On the basis of his personal experience, which he presents as a case of "self-healing", he posits a theory of five biological laws that establish the link between the mind and disease.

His essential diagnostic tool is the cerebral scanner; using it, he claims to be able to diagnose any pathology. According to Hamer, pathologies always originate in relation to a conflict, a conflict that is both biological in nature and a result of antiquated impulses. According to him, our society seeks to extinguish the impulses of the libido, and this conflict between impulse and society gives birth to disease. Hamer offers a kind of Freudian reinterpretation of psychosomatic medicine, to which he adds a technical element through the use of the cerebral scanner.

Hamer says that the scanner-reading and the patient interview enable him to identify the cerebral disease and where it is located, and also the conflicts that generated the disease: mother-child conflicts, power or territorial challenges, conflicts of a sexual nature, feelings of superiority or inferiority. He explains that each conflict occupies a specific place in the brain and generates a specific pathology. Thus, the "conflict of the nest" is located in the cerebellum, which "was in formation during the period when the mother-child conduct of mammals was programmed".

According to the "bronze law" and the "five biological laws", body organs that develop contemporaneously cohabit in the same area of the brain and are born together in the embryo, where they form part of the endoderm, the mesoderm or the ectoderm. Hamer maps the cerebral zones and the "Hamer hotspots", and establishes a correlation between these hotspots, various pathologies, and the embryonic origins of the pathologies. Thus, the "Hamer hotspots" that correspond to the malignant tumors of endodermal origin are located in the cerebral trunk, while lesions of the mesoderm correspond to the cerebellum and to the cerebral matter, and ectodermal lesions to the cerebral cortex.

Hamer's doctrines are a mix of embryogenetic data and the cerebral cartography elaborated in the 19th century by Broca. The two complementary steps of the diagnosis are the cartographic localization of the supposed cerebral lesion and the interpretation of what the patient says, to identify what conflicts are operating in him.

This is a dubious diagnostic theory at the very least, but the great leap to complete delusion is confirmed when we come to the question of how the patient should be treated. Indeed, Hamer says the first decision that must be taken is to stop accepting any medical treatment, for it interrupts the ascending phase of the disease, during which the patient is in a state of stress (in sympathicotony). After having terminated all other forms of therapy, the patient is, still according to Hamer, in a state of relaxation (vagotony), an essential phase for the healing. Then the organic lesions must heal. The "Hamer hotspot" in question is "healed", it "repairs itself" and surrounds itself with an edema — which Hamer treats with penicillin or cortico-therapy, and applications of crushed ice, while administering sedatives and anti-epileptics "to support the rest phase".

For denying the existence of cancerous metastases and carcinogenic processes, Hamer was permanently barred from medical practice in Germany in 1986. This did not prevent the ex-doctor from disseminating his ideas throughout Europe and from promoting the creation of structures like Stop Cancer, and AUBE (Association for Universal Well-Being) whose leader is Dr. Noella P., a surgeon who was suspended from her hospital functions for a six-month period, for having propagated Hamer's methods.[28]

In August 1996, Hamer made the front pages when the President of Austria, Thomas Klestil, personally had to intervene to secure the repatriation of young Olivia Pilhan. She had been "sequestered" in Spain by her parents, whom Hamer had persuaded to remove from the chemotherapy intended to treat a renal tumor. Repatriated to Austria and treated by conventional methods, the young child seems to be out of danger today.

The Pilhan scandal was revealing. Hamer was finally condemned to 19 months in jail by the court of Cologne for non-assistance to a person in danger, infringement of the legislation on alternative medicine and illegal practice of medicine. Three of his patients had died of cancer after he diverted them from traditional medicine.

The Patriarch

Addiction is one of the most lucrative markets for the healing groups or cults. The Lucien Engelmajer Association, more commonly known as The Patriarch, has made this a specialty.

Lucien Engelmajer, The Patriarch, was born in 1920 in Germany. After honorable conduct during the Second World War (he was a volunteer in the French army), he went into medical school. . . for a few months. After a career selling furniture, in 1972 he opened his first treatment center for drug addicts.

Initially, this enterprise responded to a very real need. Drug addiction had exploded since 1968 and was devastating society, it was a not-well-understood pathology and there were few therapies available. At the time, Dr. Olivenstein was almost the only one to establish a drug addict treatment center. Engelmajer responded to demand from both families and the public authorities. However, he was soon accused of misconduct, and there was a memorably virulent debate in 1977 in Lisbon, at a congress of the International Council on Addiction, between Dr. Francis Curtet and The Patriarch's disciples.

Indeed, within a few years Engelmajer's good intentions had given way to practices that are reproachable on many counts: brutal deprivation of the toxins without any substitutes or analgesics; treatment the consisted of nothing but fasting and herbal teas; "tough" psychotherapy; employing the drug addicts at tasks that are a far cry from the concept of ergo-therapy, etc.. In May 1985, the Consigny Report delivered at the request of the French government unambiguously condemned the Center:

> The Association of The Patriarch is like a foreign body in French society, not organically related to it, inspired only by its own truth, and at the same time gripped by a kind of obsession with a supposed surrounding external threat.
>
> Most of the centers were opened without any prior announcement, thus facing the authorities with a *fait accompli*.
>
> The finances of the association are ambiguous, with a lack of disclosure and, to some extent, irregularities that, deliberately or not, make it impossible to get a transparent and clear view of its management. . . .
>
> Sanitary control and medical supervision are seldom in conformity with the regulations. In certain centers, these failings are so severe as to justify their being closed immediately.

But meanwhile The Patriarch had diversified its activities. AIDS, which made inroads in the drug addict population first, appeared on the medical scene. Engelmajer recognized the deficiency of the medical and social support system once again. In 1983, it created open treatment centers for HIV-positive individuals, assisted by some researchers and biologists who considered the 3300 seropositive people (claimed by The Patriarch) an interesting pool for epidemiologic experimentation.[29]

Two associations were thus created: ADDEPOS (Association for the Rights and Duties of the AIDS-positive and AIDS-carriers), and

IDRET (European Institute for Documentation and Research on Addiction). Through these organizations, Engelmajer recruited a star, in the person of Prof. Mirko Beljanski. Since 1990, Beljanski has worked closely with The Patriarch while continuing his own medical tests. Thus, a structure that has been called a cult (by the French parliament) is in cahoots with a researcher who was convicted in 1994 of illegal practice of medicine. How many other laws are being broken?

It is true that the public authorities seem to suffer from poor vision when they examine The Patriarch's practices: they are at the very least exceptionally tolerant, in his case. Some municipalities go as far as to provide free apartments and work space to the cult, and this in spite of the investigations commissioned by the social services, the unfavorable opinions recorded by specialists in addiction and AIDS, and the legal convictions of The Patriarch.

Scientology — Narconon

Narconon, a subsidiary of Scientology, and the association "Yes to Life, No to Drugs" have also made a specialty of the fight against drugs and treating drug addicts. They push to the front of the stage such brilliant standard-bearers as Chick Corea and other well-known performers. Narconon recommends the same techniques as Scientology, which are related in my last book, *Soul Snatchers: the Mechanics of Cults*.[28]

Drug addicts are just one of the Scientologists' targets for recruitment. The offer of care and healing through techniques derived from dianetics is only a come-on. The detoxification of the patient by means of "dianetics purification" is more a matter of manipulation, through the general weakening that it causes; it is a way of brainwashing the subject.

Frequently convicted for illegal practice of medicine, violence, fraud and slander, the Scientologists have more and more trouble getting people to accept their techniques as effective health measures, as they like to claim. They recommend their purification processes to eliminate X-rays and nuclear radiation, and to treat goiter and warts, hypertension and psoriasis, hemorrhoids and myopia. . . why would anyone find that hard to swallow?

Scientology has built a library of several hundreds of volumes of writings exalting the effects of purification, and its disciples spew propaganda based on irresponsible medical writings by doctors who are more interested in the support provided by Scientology than in their patients' well-being. On the other hand, responsible scientific reviews have long since "eliminated" dianetics and purification from the lists of therapies — relegating them to the great bazaar of medical fraud.

14. THE FOUNDATIONS OF PATAMEDICINE

Oh, fire of the Spirit Paraclet, life of the life of any creature, you are holy, you who vivify all forms. You are holy, you who anoint with balm our deepest fractures, you are holy, you who staunch our stinking wounds.

The Abbess of Rupertsberg, 1147.

Nothing is more dogmatically certain than the possible sanctification of human action.

Teilhard de Chardin,
The Divine Milieu.

Inventorying and analyzing patamedicines and the theories behind them shows how severely the rational mind can be paralyzed by the desire of the patients — and even those who are in good health — "to believe".

Medical charlatans do not base their claims on scientific proof but, quite to the contrary, on peremptory assertions — the kind of assertions that they challenge when they come out of the mouths of those who defend "real" medicine.

Most of the offers to provide experimental verification of patamedicine are never carried out — and for good reason. In some cases, the pataphysicians have agreed to abide by the verdict of the experiments. That didn't turn out so well for them: as we have seen, double-blind testing of homeopathy and acupuncture led to the discrediting of these techniques. It is understandable that other pata-physicians refuse to yield to the demands of proper scientific experimental protocols.

The attitude that the pataphysicians take is something like that of the folks who believe in mind-reading and psycho-kinesis. In these two cases (whether it we are talking about transmitting mind-waves or bending little spoons), the experiments are convincing when they are conducted without rigorous controls, but they fall short when the witnesses are able to observe them very closely. The "believers" "explain" any scams that may be revealed by saying that the behavior of the inspectors disturbed the medium or the parapsychologist, and therefore the experiment was not conducted under proper conditions. A parapsychologist, caught "red-handed", may admit having cheated but he will say that it was only in order to protect his image, and his supposed powers are never questioned by the "believers". (It is interesting to note that Uri Geller's ability to move and to remotely bend spoons by the force of his thought-waves alone were described as juggling acts by the illusionist James Randi, who later also emphasized the lack of scientific rigor in Jacques Beneveniste's protocols.)

The second argument that pataphysicians like to use, when they are caught, is that the phenomena underlying their pata-technical effects are too subtle to be registered by laboratory measuring instruments, which they say are too crude to detect cosmic or bio-dynamic forces. Given the lack of critical thinking exhibited by their followers, the pataphysicians have a merry time presenting their techniques as universal answers to every question on physical or psychic health.

An Act of Faith

Patamedicine is essentially a sign of absolute belief in principles that most often arise from a cosmo-divine interpretation of what it is to be human; the constantly drawn parallels between microcosm and macrocosm reflects this. References to esoteric data such as the Emerald Tablet give the beliefs a veneer of historical pseudo-veracity and creates a supposed traditional heritage. Historical medical references (the medicine of the Pharaohs, of the wise Indians, of eternal China) are woven in to strengthen the belief.

Charcot had already analyzed man's propensity to believe in a miraculous form of healing in 1897, and, reading his work, one sees that nothing in this field has changed in a hundred years.

> The so-called miracles have a double nature. They are generated by a special disposition of the patient's mind: confidence, credulity, suggestibility, as we say today, which are constitutive of faith-healing [the faith that heals], which is active in varying degrees in different people.
>
> Generally, faith-healing does not develop spontaneously in all its healing intensity. A patient hears people say that in such and such a sanctuary, miraculous healings are taking place. . . . He questions the people he knows, and requests information in full detail on the marvelous cures about which he hears such rumors. He hears only encouraging words, not only from his own direct acquaintances, but often even from his doctor. The doctor does not want to take away from his patient the last ray of hope . . . In any event, any contradiction at this point would only serve to exalt the patient's belief in the possibility of a miracle cure. Faith-healing starts to take shape, it grows, it incubates, and the pilgrimage to be achieved becomes an obsession. . . .Under these conditions, it is not long before the mental state dominates the physical state. . . . One last effort: immersion in a special pool, some formal worship, and faith-healing produces the desired effect; the miracle cure becomes a reality.[1]

Miracle Cures

For pataphysicians, faithful followers bearing witness to their healing are like manna from heaven. All practitioners of alternative, natural or traditional medicine have up their sleeves a personal experience to relate, proving the cogency of such and such technique. In November 1993, the Association of Life and Action held a conference entirely devoted to this topic, under the title: "They were called incurable, and yet. . . !" All the testimonies are impressing in their sincerity and they reflect real suffering; but they are the quintessence of medical obscurantism:

> Now, when I see somebody who has had a nervous breakdown, I say to myself: "What is necessary at all costs, above all, is not to go to a neurologist, and especially not to take any medications, but to try to come out of it yourself by living a healthy life. And then to get plenty of exercise, to go out, to lead a healthy life. That is what is important."[2]

Today's misgivings about synthetic molecules is deeply exploited to cast discredit upon official medicine in the favor of such and such patamedicine. Efforts to promote patamedicine frequently use artifices such as references to the phenomena of immunity — especially given the fear caused by AIDS, which results in an attack on the immune system. Through a skilful and misleading amalgam, official medicine is thus associated with the development of major pathologies. The intellectual game is complete: according to patamedical logic, it is the official doctor who is responsible for AIDS!

> Drugs have the same effect. From the first moment when you go to see the doctor, the neurologist, who supposedly cures the mind, from the moment he gives you a little pill, he induces in you something very serious . . . When we talk about immunosuppression, AIDS, etc., think of all the medications that were given to you since early childhood: cough syrup — that we give to little babies so they won't cough — contains alcohol and real drugs. . . And you have, there, one of the essential bases of the suppression of the immune system, first of all, and secondly, of the tendency that the child will then develop to look toward artificial drugs and chemical paradises. And it is medicine that creates that, it is our synthetic agro-alimentary habit that produces it.[3]

Another artifice is the constant reference to the "power of love". This fuels the growth of healing groups, for whom love equals healing. Patamedicine exploits people's natural tendency to Manicheism: opposing the natural and the artificial, then love and the artificial, and finally by making "artificial" a synonym of hatred and death.

> If the child is breast-fed and loved by his family, if he is not given anti-biological products, from today's commercial trade, if he is not stuffed with chemicals, if he is not made aware of drugs, there are very few reasons for him to go into drugs on his own.

> Study the kids on drugs. Often, they were medicated since very early childhood; they were drugged.

> Then we say of those young people: "We have to put them in prison, keep them out of trouble, etc." But who is it that we should be locking up, to keep them from making trouble? I will not answer you![4]

In the public testimony orchestrated by pataphysicians, obscurantism and hysterical belief are the rules. Sometimes, when such a profession of faith comes from a doctor, it becomes criminal:

> I'd like to say a word about AIDS. There are people who have AIDS, these days. It is always the same: they come to me when they are at the end of the rope, when they have nowhere else to turn. I have, for example, two young people in the late stages of AIDS, i.e. confined to bed, with muscular atrophy, piles of things like that, who have taken not a few different drugs. . . After applying naturopathy for a certain period, one of the two people ran a temperature of 105-106° for 27 days. 27 days!

> I counseled him, and he stopped taking anything. We dropped everything: AZT, DDI, the injections, antibiotics — especially Bactrim which, by the way, in my view, is a deadly antibiotic, but in any case, well, that is personal — but we dropped everything.[5]

Given such testimony, from a doctor hallowed with the prestige of being the one who "knows", it is astonishing that the authorities of the medical profession did not crack down. Wasn't this a case of failing to come to the assistance of a person in danger?

The Pataphysician as the New Priest of Healing

Consciously or not, most believers in patamedicine invest those who are "treating" them with "magical powers" that to some extent resemble religiosity. The way healers, teachers of patamedicine and holistic doctors are perceived implies that the function is quasi-holy in nature. One acquires the capacity to cure by purifying oneself, by initiating oneself through a quest that is as much mystical as it is medical. This status as an initiate, as a link between the divine and the human, is openly asserted by some — such as Maud Pison, a self-proclaimed reincarnation of the Virgin — and more discretely by others.

Thus Maguy Lebrun, who has been the leading light behind prayer and healing groups for several years, declares that he is "only" the channel of an angel. And for still others, being a doctor is equivalent to a sacerdotal state that implies membership in the caste of priests.

Luc Jouret, whose name is now attached to the Order of the Solar Temple massacres, once declared in a television broadcast:

> In all great civilizations, we note that the doctors were always priests and vice versa. . . . I am convinced. . . that a doctor who is not concerned with reinstating himself in a dimension where the spirit takes precedence over matter cannot understand his patient as such. And that is pretty much what is happening in medicine today; without denigrating the very real value that it has contributed in the transformation of man, it remains nevertheless true that it leads to a dead end . . . because it refuses to integrate spiritual man into physical man, even though it was spiritual man that shaped physical man . . . .[6]

Therapeutic power plus the sacerdotal function confer on certain physicians and pataphysicians an aura of credibility and the appearance of being "spiritual guides". The holistic discourse and its holy dimension are at the heart of this medical-spiritual approach, and little by little the physician or the pataphysician is invested with supernatural and divine powers that make them the spiritual heirs of the priest-doctors and shamans.

The sacerdotal dimension may be unspoken or it may be clearly asserted, as in the case of the Family of Nazareth. It explains the absolute power that often is conferred on the practitioner, who is regarded as possessing the gift of healing but also a power of control over the acts of daily life. Religious discourse is woven into the spiel of many medical patatechnicians who thus inscribe themselves in a theological tradition that may be recognized (prayer and healing groups), deviant (Family of Nazareth) or apostatic. This pseudo-religiosity is used, in fact, to mask the development of a cult.

Healing by the Masters

Spontaneous healing by the guru, the leader or the teacher is one of the points in common between the various spiritual healing groups. It's best if the founder of the group has cured himself of a serious disease. So far, cancer has embodied the "supreme" disease, the disappearance of which has been seen as a sign of divine or at least supernatural intervention. There is good reason to bet that AIDS will soon supplant cancer as the disease to be cured in these Masters' patter.

In 1862, Mary Baker Eddy, founder of Christian Science, was relieved of diffuse pains in the spinal column and the abdomen by an act of telepathy performed by a mental healer, Phineas P. Quimby. Closer to our times, Claire Nuer proclaims to all and sundry that she was cured of a melanoma of the eye in 1982 by a technique inspired by Carl

Simonton. Her mystical healing has become a sales tool for The Heart of Communication, an association that offers both health and personal growth.

In 1975, Martin Brofman, a 34-year-old and a healer, teacher and writer, suffered from a cancerous tumor of the spinal cord. He discovered the power of the mind, and cured himself spontaneously. Astonished by his own healing, he studied the relationships between consciousness, visual energy and health, spiritual imbalance and disease. He created the World Institute of Technologies for Healing (WITH), then the Body Mirror System of Healing Workshop, which is largely inspired by energy medicine and the theory of chakras.

> The parts of your body that do not function well reflect the parts of your life that are not functioning well. When there is tension in a particular part of your body, it reflects a particular tension in one part of your consciousness concerning a particular part of your life. . . .

> Energy runs through our being and it is directed by our thoughts, our feelings, our desires. When we block the flow of energy through an inharmonious interaction with our environment, the results are disease, accidents, certain types of symptoms. We can then say that any disease, any accident results from energy blocks. Since we direct our energy, or our consciousness, with our thoughts, we have the capacity to resolve energy where it has been blocked, in ourselves or others.

> When we do this, the result is a return to the experience of completeness. Healing occurs. We believe that everything can be cured. It is only a question of knowing how.

> The Body Mirror System is a technology that explores how.[7]

But Brofman is not satisfied with curing cancer, he is able to restore the sight of blind men.

Medicine acknowledges that it has met its match, but Martin Brofman, through a series of chance occurrences, discovered the powers
of mind control and body control through the Alpha state, and something incredible occurred: one year later, he was cured! . . .

This phenomenon stimulated him to conduct research on the link
between awareness and eyesight, spiritual imbalance and disease.
His results have already helped many people in the United States and
in Europe to improve their eyesight, to get rid of their glasses and to
cure their bodies and souls. Since then, he has been teaching these
techniques, so powerful, that he used on himself with success.[8]

In 1997, one of Brofman's disciples, a graduate of WITH, was convicted and fined $5,000 for false advertising likely to mislead the con-
sumer. One of his students, who had multiple sclerosis, had filed a
complaint after taking a course in body-mirror training, saying that she
did not see her condition improving. But Brofman had proclaimed to
her: "Only faith saves, healing is an expression of love. All can be
cured". . . (as long as you are not ill).

The Body as a Holy Tabernacle, or The Origins of Medical Obscurantism

The question of how the soul and body are related has fed debates
on the innate and the acquired, the material and the spiritual, since the
17th century.

Since Hippocrates and Galen, one of the principle questions for
the doctor was to define the role of the organs, and to figure out where
the emotions and the soul were located. The Church's prohibition of
dissection limited man's knowledge of anatomy. In the Middle Ages,
on the basis of clandestine autopsies, anatomists finally were able to
describe the cerebral ventricles. The Church bans were backed up by
burnings at the stake, so that medical obscurantism was preferred by
far over any systematic study of human anatomy and physiology, which

might have called into question the Church teachings. Faith and the desire for knowledge clashed head-on, and only small clusters of scientists bore up under the pressure — such as the University of Montpellier, in the south of France.

In 1215, the Lateran Council made it a crime for priests and monks to practice surgery, on the grounds that "the Church abhors blood". Nonetheless, clerics continued practicing their art, in secret. In the 10th, 11th and 12th centuries, Arabs and Jews became the only agents who could transmit medical knowledge, and their influence managed to break the constraints of the church by invading first the Spanish universities, then those of southern France.

It is generally accepted that autopsies were non-existent until the middle of the 13th century. Anatomy was studied using animals, primarily the pig. The first implicit authorization of the autopsy is probably the edict of Frederic II in 1240. Hitherto, the holy nature of the human body forbade practitioners from prying into an area reserved to the divine and from revealing the secrets of life. The existence of a divine principle of life was accepted and beyond discussion — as it still is, nowadays, for many believers and for users of patamedicine.

Alternative Medicines and Ancient Religions

It is no mere coincidence if holistic medicine to some extent derives its name from "holy" as well as through reference to the whole organism, holos ("the whole"). In olden times, the power of healing was assigned to the holder of the religious function.

Cave walls bear the traces of ceremonies where propitiatory acts and rites intermingle with invocations of the "gods" or the powers that governed the cosmos and its inhabitants. The Sumerians, 5000 years before Christ, inscribed their magic experiments and their formulas on clay tablets. Among them, many refer to medical problems that were treated through religious ritual — although purely medical techniques were also used.

In 1921, Sir William Osler, a pioneer of British medicine, called the Egyptian Imhotep "the first doctor to step out of the mists of proto-history" and he individualized him amongst the figures of the Egyptian pantheon, where he had been considered, until then, to be a mythical divinity. With some difficulty, Osler managed to draw a line between the medical practices of Imhotep and the religious practices of his peers.

By studying the Ebers and Smith papyruses, written 1500 and 2000 years BC, respectively, we can be certain that the Egyptian doctors had a diagnostic science based on clinical signs, that they could precisely identify various symptoms and diseases, that they recommended treatment — often suitable — for these pathologies, and that they knew how to prepare some 900 remedies. However, it is equally clear that the medical practice of the time was not entirely dissociated from the religious view of disease. For example, the Ebers papyrus talks of ophthalmology, identifying disorders like trachoma, abscess, entropion and hemeralopia; the clinical observations are similar to today's, but the papyrus invokes a divine epic where the gods play the roles of doctor and patient. Thus, the god Râ checks the god Horus's eyesight by asking him to read hieroglyphs on the wall, first with one eye, then with the other, not unlike today's tests. The Egyptian doctors' treatises are strewn with invocations to the gods, with prayers and references to the cycle of the Nile and to astrological entities. In spite of the advanced degree of knowledge — including the early discovery of antibiotics — to justify itself, Egyptian medicine still needed to refer to the gods and their powers.

Greece did much the same, by ascribing to the gods the power to dominate life, health and death through their Olympian misadventures. This influence is still seen in the Oath of Asclepiades, written one century before our era. With some revisions, it became the Hippocratic oath, and then that sworn by today's doctors.

I swear by Apollo the doctor, Asclepius, Hygeia and Panakeia, taking as witness all the gods and all the goddesses, to fulfill this oath and this written engagement to the fullest extent of my power and my judgment. . .

I will prescribe dietetic regimens to the advantage of my patients to the best of my ability and my judgment.

In whatever house I must enter, I will go there for the service of the patients, avoiding any voluntary misdeed or corrupting action, most particularly avoiding any lascivious bodily contact with women or men, be they free or slaves.

The things that I may see or hear, in practicing or even outside the practice of my art, concerning the lives of individuals, that should not be revealed to the outside, I will conceal, considering that those things are entitled to the status of secrecy of the mysteries.

If I shall fulfill this oath and do it honor until the end, let it be given to me to enjoy the fruits of life and this art, honored forever among all men. But if I violate them and if I perjure myself, let the opposite happen.

Only modern times could make us give up these references to gods — for the more prosaic reference to "Masters", those mandarins who seem to rule over our medical future, who may, in fact, be more fearsome than the gods.

While the Egyptians were writing the Ebers papyrus, the Assyrians were giving Gilgamesh (legendary founder of the royal dynasty) the power to sow illness and death among his people — but also to give them life, thanks to the holy herbs that he searched out to save his companion Enkodu and thus to bring immortality to the earth.

From 1027 to 256 BC, the Chou dynasty reigned in China, and it is from these times that the principal Chinese traditional medical works such as the Chen-Nong Pen Tsao, or *The Book of the Divine Worker*, which enumerates poisons and their antidotes. But it was also under their reign that Confucius revealed the importance of deifying the doctor: "the man whose character is unstable cannot become a shaman." When the medicine of simple people fails, they have nothing left to turn to but exorcisms and magic, the only consolation against the aggressions of fate.

In those days, acupuncture was not yet as systematized as it later was: its arrows, which became needles, were used to drive out and to destroy demons who were thought to invade the patient's body — this suggests a continuity of ideas from the depictions found in cave paintings.

Across the Pacific, Peruvian civilizations also had their godly doctors. In 1000 BC, the Chavin civilization had its priest-doctors, who provided care thanks to the powers that they received from the Jaguar god. For the Mochicas, life was determined by the outcome of battles between the Jaguar god and the Serpent god, and when physical treatments failed, the role of the shaman-doctor was to win over one or the other through his prayers.[9]

Thus, from Antiquity to the present day, medicine and religion have been closely connected in the prescriptions by which man looks after his body and soul. These are the same prescriptions that are gaining strength again today in fields that are as much a matter of religions as of cult practices.

Pentecostalists and Divine Healing

Since the advent of Christianity, healing has been taken as the sign of baptism in the Holy Ghost. Jesus Christ cured lepers and revived the dead: after him, his disciples were satisfied to relieve pain and to cure the most common diseases. Invested with the power of the Spirit by anointment with holy oil, the kings of France had the gift of curing scrofula.

To the Pentecostalists, baptism in the Holy Spirit confers on believers gifts or particular charismas — speaking in tongues (more prosaically called jargonaphasy by the psychiatrists), the gift of prophecy and that of divine healing. This charismatic aspect has infiltrated the Catholic Church in recent years, and the Church must fight back. In this dynamics, the pentecostalist and charismatic groups attribute special gifts to their leaders — their pastors are supposed to possess powers of healing. This movement started up in the 18th century, beginning with the practices of the Reverend John Wesley, who saw the sanctification of the subject as a different act from conversion. Pentecostalist, charismatic or revivalist groups are characterized by group meetings where singing, invocations, public confessions, dancing, etc., leads the group into an actual collective trance, which makes possible the "healing" of hysterical subjects who "come back to life" under the eyes of the group, thanks to the dramatic intensity of the meetings and their high degree of collective affect. Even though the movement originated in Protestantism, the great majority of pentecostalist groups refuse to affiliate with any of the major religions, thus avoiding any close scrutiny of their practices which are basically a form of group dynamics, at best.

Sin, Karma and Disease

Through the doctrines of karma, Buddhism and Hinduism teach that man undergoes a destiny over which he certainly can have some influence, but which comprises many elements that are unchangeable. The karmic vision of disease, taken up by so many contemporary cults, is the most frequent derivative of occidentalized and poorly interpreted Buddhism.

Since Antiquity, disease has often been depicted as the result of a fault, of a sin. Facial angioma (the wine spot) was long regarded as a sign of the devil. Many sanctuaries of the ancient world were dedicated to the healing gods. And while Judaism reports few accounts of healing, it does put in the mouth of Isaiah the words that evoke the Messiah's power of healing. Jesus would cure those who were ill. But he would do so upon one condition, that of faith: "Believe in me and you will be cured." From the very start, healing and faith were thus interdependent, but at the same time sin and disease were made synonymous.

Healings are not only physiological acts, they are signs of the arrival of the Messiah, a revelation from God or the essence of the prophet. Then, as a side-effect, illness automatically becomes a sign of the evil one, a sign of sin, making the patient responsible for his condition and to blame for both his disease and his sin. "If I with the finger of God cast out devils, no doubt the kingdom of God is come upon you." (Luke 11:20). Healing was, in fact, a low-level exorcism.

In the current revival of ritual healing within charismatic groups, and through the propagation of karmic concepts in those cults that look to Buddhist, Hindu or theosophic sources, the role of offering a doctor's ministrations is transferred to the pastor or to the guru. The esoteric language of the cults serves to create and maintain the confusion between the field of the psyche and that of the spirit.

However, if illness is invested with spiritualistic connotations and made into an expression of the individual's failings, or bad karma that has to be expiated, it is not because the disease has any psychic origin or because medical wisdom shows it to be a psychosomatic pathology. Disease has always been a favorite field for guru-healers; indeed, once the body is weakened, the mind is much more inclined to accept the fables that are offered as supposed cures.

Denunciations of Official Medicine's Alleged Abuses

An atmosphere of medical catastrophism that seems to pick up the echoes of those fears of global conspiracies lends support to the growth of patamedicine. One such association, led by a doctor who opposes routine vaccinations, put out a brochure calling for "genuine health care policies" that would

> . . . stop poisoning the populace and generating appalling medical catastrophes with therapies that are more dangerous than the diseases they are supposed to treat, and vaccination campaigns that amount to actual genocide, more or less intentional; avoiding controlling the population by imaginary terror campaigns that are entirely fabricated and that are amplified by a medical profession that has lost all common sense and all measure.[10]

Very often, this kind of denunciation of alleged abuses plays on contemporary fears and develops a perverse series of arguments built on known failures of science that are held up as irrefutable proof that contemporary medical practices are no good.

> [Following a vaccination] there is a risk of contamination from:
>
> 1. viruses that are as yet unknown. This has already occurred and is still occurring with the vaccines against polio (virus SV 40 or STL V3), yellow fever (hepatitis B) or influenza in particular;
> 2. by prions (mad cow disease);
> 3. by carcinogenic substances;
> 4. by carcinogenic or mutagenic foreign nucleic acids (with the risk of birth defects, which amount to deformities and death in the descent).
> 5. Any foreign substance inoculated into the organism across its natural barriers necessarily sets off a reaction from the organism, to reject the intruder. This intrusion breaks down the immune system and throws it into disarray, opening the door to AIDS and to the degenerative diseases that are literally exploding these days: cancer, multiple sclerosis, rheumatism, diabetes, insulin-dependencies, and all the auto-immune diseases.[11]

In spite of the undeniable strides made by medicine, in spite of the declining death rates due to preventive vaccines and improvements in hygiene, such arguments continue to convince the fringes of society, and are taken as signs of the unquestionable goodwill of certain cults.

Thus, the Horus Cult is happy to produce fake certificates for the vaccine against tetanus. And Tabitha's Place, by refusing a surgical operation for a new-born baby under the pretext of respecting divine will, had no qualms about condemning to death a young child who was born with a cardiac malformation.

Patamedicine, Magic, and the Third Way

Between belief in divine healing and confidence in a completely mechanistic scientific process, patamedicine represents a third way that is basically a primitive belief in magic. Absolute confidence in God or in a doctor removes the patient from any active role in deciding how to deal with his condition, as his illness evolves. By contrast, patamedical magic gives the patient back an active part in the process of his healing.

While magic may originally have meant the practices of the sacerdotal caste of the Medes, who were followers of pseudo-sciences such as astrology or hermetic medicine, the word gradually has taken on a broader meaning to encompass beliefs and practices that have little to do with the rites of organized worship and that presuppose a belief in supernatural forces immanent in nature.[11]

For this reason, patamedicine always presupposes the belief in a principle that "animates" the human being and that explains the "inexplicable" aspects of physiology. Energy, in Chinese medicine, or white holes in the memory of water, all derive from this basic approach. Patamedics accept the whole gamut of magical approaches to health. They calibrate their responses to health questions and propose to the patient techniques that gradually move away from the scientific approach and move closer and closer to religious belief, even faith.

Some ethnologists, like Frazer, saw magic as a form of prescience, for this practice includes references to determinism. Frazer described two principles in magical belief, two principles that agree with certain laws of the association of ideas and that are found in patamedicine — even if they may not be overtly stated.

The principle of similarity says that the similar calls the similar, like goes to like. Thus, every practice that has been observed as being simultaneous to an effect is considered to be an inductive principle — and reproducing the practice is expected to generate the same effect. *The principle of contiguity*, the second principle, states that things that once were in contact continue to act upon each other even after the contact has ceased. Thus, in magic, a photograph is an extension of the being that was photographed, and magic that is practiced on the photo will have its effect upon the individual. Any action on the material object will affect the whole person.

Homeopathy is a perfect illustration of the principle of similarity. It is all the harder to criticize since it seems to respect the scientific laws of causality. But to accept the principle of similarity as flawless scientific reasoning means maintaining confusion between an action and the sign of an action. A green light is not what makes motor vehicles start moving after a red light. It merely signals some events that take place contemporaneously. In the same vein, when a person recovers after such and such technique has been applied, that is not absolute proof that the technique was valid. Only verification of the chain of cause and effect is proof of the authenticity of the phenomenon observed, even if the phenomenon is repeated several times. The fact that the sun reaches the zenith at midday and the fact that everyone's watches and clocks point to the numeral 12 are not part of a chain of cause and effect on each other — even though the coincidence seems to hold true universally. . . . until daylight savings time, when we change our schedules. And so it is not, as the homeopaths claim, because quinine creates malaria-like symptoms in healthy people that quinine has a beneficial effect on those who already exhibit the symptoms of malaria. The principle of similarity is a magic virtuality, and is not consistent with scientific thought.

The principle of contiguity is widespread in the world of patamedicine, from tele-therapy to the various diagnostic techniques that rely on photographs, or the Kirlian effect. In astrology, predictive numerology and the techniques of morphopsychology (which are sinisterly reminiscent of the Third Reich's Institute of Anthropology) all reflect this principle. A given astrological sign, a given birth number, a given physical characteristic is supposed to be either the generating principle (astrology) or an identifying sign (numerology, or a physical sign in morphopsychology) of the psychological nature of the individual and of his destiny.

Contrary to religion, which grants almighty power to the divine, magic thought allows us to keep some partial power over matter, and in fact over the phenomena of health and healing; it is based on a form of determinism and rests on the belief in the existence of supernatural, suprahuman, but non-divine forces.

Magic thought shares with scientific thought a certainty about the course of predetermined sequences of events. While prayer may be intended to secure divine intervention in the processes of mystical healing, in the practice of magic this intervention is not necessary. The magical action is supposed to secure the desired effect on its own, and for this reason magic and science have the same goal: to gain control over how things turn out. Medical magic and medicine share one thing: the certainty of taking some action against the disease.

Magic and science differ, however, in how they analyze their successes and failures. If the magical practice ends in failure, there is no retrospective analysis of the failure. The act of magic implies repeating *ad libitum* the same action, no matter how it turns out. On the contrary, scientific thought follows a trial-and-error approach, until it achieves trial-and-success, and any failure requires an analysis that can lead to changes of operational methods.

Herein lies the great deficiency of patamedicine. It refuses to learn from its failures and claims that any failure must be the result of the technique having been applied poorly. In patamedicine, failure does not mean that the theory is faulty but that it was put into practice in the wrong way. There is no learning by experience, and no revising or adjusting of the theory, although that is how science progresses.

Marcel Mauss, an anthropologists who studied the phenomenon of magic, stressed the important role played in the ceremonial process by the notion of a supernatural force that only magic could control; he compared it to the Melanesians' "mana".[12] In patamedicine, this force is omnipresent, and is the foundation of the magical-therapeutic act performed by the practitioner. Belief in the existence of this "mana" places the pataphysician in the position of a creator or a super-actor in the realm of health. The pataphysician is supposed to possess the ability to act and to create: he is a link between man and the divine. This holy power enables the magus to acquire broader powers in the other spheres of human activity and to a large extent explains the power of the guru-doctor and the tendency of these groups to degenerate into cults.

The Esoteric Bases of Patamedicine

In reaction against the mechanistic approach to patients and their concerns, some authors defend alternative medicines by claiming that their profession is rooted in esoteric practices. Dr. Michaud, a homeopathic doctor, is one of them. He sets homeopathy in an esoteric context that defies common sense and the most rudimentary verification.

> By tradition, esoteric knowledge is transmitted through the path of the initiate, from master to disciple. This initiatory knowledge is quite different from the deductive knowledge that is the foundation

of science. It is generally acknowledged that esotericism also aims to uncover the hidden meanings of things and that consequently it requires research.[14]

Dr. Michaud sees esoteric medicine (and homeopathy, which he considers to be related to esoteric medicine) as being founded on three fundamental laws: the law of analogy, the rhythmic law and the ternary (three-fold) law of balance.

The law of analogy to which Michaud (and nearly every pataphysician) refers is one of the constants of esotericism. It is anchored in ancient writings, and traces its origins to the god Thot — in his transformation as an oracle, represented by Hermès Trismégiste. (See the traditions of the Rosicrucians, Meister Eckhart, etc..) The law is expressed through the Emerald Tablet: "True, without error, certain and most true: that which is above is as that which is below, and that which is below is as that which is above, to perform the miracles of the One Thing." It establishes a similarity of essence and action between the microcosmic universe and the macrocosmic universe. It is the base of spagyric and alchemical medicine and it clarifies the theories of medical astrology.

In the approach constituted by the negation of organic and biological causes of disease (or their relegation constitutes to secondary importance, the vision of a cosmic nature sees disease as a sign of cosmic responsibility for the patient. To be sick becomes a betrayal of the cosmic order, or the fulfillment of it. In the former case, the patient is guilty; in the second, he is impotent vis-à-vis his destiny. However, these pataphysicians ignore certain contradictions that arise from the theoretical bases of their practices.

The rhythmic law draws a parallel between the vital cycles and the planetary cycles. In patamedicine, woman's cycle of ovulation reproduces the twenty-eight day lunar cycle. This might bode ill for the continuity of the celestial mechanics, given the irregular cycles of many women — and it is even more alarming, if you consider the stages of adolescence or menopause.

The law of ternary balance rests on the traditional symbolism of the number 3, which is explained in esoteric medicine by the assertion that the physical body is composed of three sections: head/throat/ abdomen, which matches a cosmic ternarity: astral body/physical body/ etheric body, and a chrono-biologic ternarity: child/adult/old person.

Needless to say, 3 is not enough for every pataphysician. Some see the number 4 as the real expression of the truth: head/throat/abdomen/ limbs; astral body/physical body/etheric body/ subtle body; infant/ child/adult/old person. For others, only the number 5, the traditional symbol of man inscribed within the pentagon, reflects the medical truth.

But then, as life expectancy keeps going up with every new generation, are we going to have to face ever large numbers, ever more complex laws of balance? I am afraid so.

15. The Authorities vs. the Charlatans

What Role Should the Authorities Play?

The medical profession has been contaminated by cults and it is difficult to assess the disorder that is created by the effects of alternative medicine techniques and by the theories that they promulgate. The French National Order of Physicians studied the phenomenon and produced a report in 1996, to alert the regional and state councils to certain trends that were becoming increasingly difficult to control.

Understandably, the atmosphere that surrounds anything that has been judged "abnormal" becomes highly charged and emotional, which often makes it difficult to make any objective analyses; and this also must be taken into account when we look at the particular psychological context of many cult victims as well as their families, who are always very traumatized.

Freedom of thought and of belief is guaranteed to our citizens, including, of course, doctors. The medical oversight authorities can only challenge a doctor when his practices run contrary to accepted medical knowledge and practices. But one has to question anyone who is morally responsible for a reprehensible act, as when a doctor who is fully cognizant of the gravity of one of his patients' conditions, and sends him off to a medical or patamedical quack or charlatan.

The authorities note that an alarming number of doctors seem to have links with cults, perhaps as many as 3,000 in France alone. However, these estimates are necessarily vague, considering how hard it is to draw a line between cult members and "sympathizers"; and it is even harder to draw a line between cult activities and certain practices of alternative medicine — not to mention the ongoing confusion between physicians and illegal practitioners.

In fact, the authorities stress the need to highlight the complicity that exists between the harmful activities of cults and certain medical practices, especially since there are doctors who become cult victims and, like any cult member, quickly become active participants in the cult phenomenon, by promoting the activities of "healing" cults or by offering their services within the context of another sort of cult.

A doctor is vulnerable to cults and medical charlatanism, like every one else, but it is critically important to note what role he is playing, given that he has great influence over his patient; and his role varies depending on whether he is the one soliciting clients or is the bait by which clients are seduced.

Doctors who allow themselves to be used as bait are actors in the general process of cult recruitment. Doctors go into cults for very ordinary reasons: they may be weakened, anxious, depressed by their impotence in the face of suffering and death. Whatever ideals the group may promote, the doctor is won over first of all by the conviviality, the warmth, the listening of the cult members; and the cult offers him new answers to his life questions or provides a sheltered realm in which he can practice his unorthodox techniques that might not be widely accepted outside of the cult, or that might be attacked as charlatanism.

Doctors who seduce clients on their own behalf are a different story; and doctors who join a cult often becomes a recruiting agent who lures in their patients and close associates. The prestige of being a doctor is an ideal "masking" situation that allows him to be in contact with and to set up potential followers, making them more open and receptive. Then it becomes possible to prescribe products promoted by a cult, and to recommend that a patient, in the interest of his personal growth and unfoldment or in the interest of treating his disease, follow the lessons and practices of a "healing"cult. This also happens in the ancillary medical professions (physical therapy, nursing, etc.) and other health-related professions (such as dentistry).

Although the authorities are paying increasing attention to the phenomenon of cult infiltration into the medical profession, they display a lukewarm optimism in noting that such incidents are fortunately not very frequent but that conclusive examples do exist. In addition, they emphasize that many doctors, for want of information (and a critical mind), allow themselves to be misled by the advertisements of pseudo-scientific treatments disseminated by cults, of which they are liable to become followers without even realizing it.

But the extension of such practices, and of "cult solicitation" by doctors, generally imply that doctors are actively involved in the activities of various cults, whether in "healing" groups or in various other cult-like movements.

There is a whole continuum ranging from movements whose principle stated objective is therapeutic (and who generally reject all traditional medicine) and certain movements that preach miracle cures as an adjunct to their general theory. The preferred prey targeted by these movements are people who suffer from incurable pathologies and, for the cults with psychoanalytical or psychological overtones, people who are avid for the potential of personal development.

Doctors' participation includes prescribing and using "medicaments" and other esoteric products or techniques, whose value is, of course, enhanced by the medical "imprimatur" which is thus conferred upon them — and this prescription goes hand in hand with the systematic rejection of traditional medicine. Sometimes this conduct is driven by idealistic motivations, but more often purely mercantile considerations are at play, either for personal enrichment or to benefit the cult by enhancing its credibility through the treatments provided.

The collusion between cult practices and medical practices are usually hidden voluntarily; and the same holds true for the "consulting" doctors to whom potential followers are addressed for a "second opinion" and often the prescription of a "method" dispensed by the cult. Some doctors who "sympathize" with these movements have been accused (rightly) of actively, if discreetly, supporting harmful cult practices when they have been publicly exposed and attacked. Several practitioners have been convicted for having proselytized on behalf of one cult or another.

European authorities have taken a firm stand. They strongly denounce the relationships between certain "soft" or alternative medicines and cults, relationships that are very clear in some cases. Alternative medicines and pseudo-medicines are often preached and used inside cults, and there is considerable danger in the fact that alternative and pseudo-scientific therapies are promoted by associations or groups known to serve as "screens" for cults.

Similarities between Cults and Alternative Medicine

In many cases, there are clear parallels between alternative medicines and cult practices, and their guiding principles are often very similar (both may reject scientific medicine, both may lean toward "orientalist" and/or "ecological" notions, etc.) and the psychological profiles and the aspirations of patient-cult members and doctors are often closely comparable.

In the general context of alternative medicines, the border is difficult to establish between tolerable and harmful prescriptions (whether active or passive — by rejecting recognized forms of treatment), and between appropriate and charlatanesque practices. In certain cases, a possible relationship should also be suspected between esoteric, pseudo-scientific medical practices and cult activities that are harmful in their own right.

It may be time for a general reminder of the guiding principles that come from the "*Primum non nocere*" and the Hippocratic oath:

> The doctor's role is to contribute to maintaining the health (the physical, moral and social well-being) of his patients and to respect their autonomy, to oppose point by point the goals of coercive cults, which are harmful to their followers. In the pursuit of his occupation, the doctor is called upon (and is given the privilege) to penetrate the intimacy of the life of his patients. In no case should he abuse it.

Various incidents have been reported, personally implicating doctors, directly or indirectly, in reprehensible practices of cult groups. If a doctor takes part in any activity that destroys someone's health, disavowing the commitments he has made, he should not be able to claim clemency on the basis of his profession. On the contrary, his status as an "expert" should mean all the more vigorous sanctions against him.

Cult influence on education and child care, with the parents' full assent, is alarming; and evidence frequently comes to light of active or passive complicity by doctors who live within these cults, performing professionally condemnable acts (faking certificates of vaccination, for example, or failing to censure physical abuse and maltreatment of children).

Other doctors have taken part in attacking the physical integrity of the followers of certain cults and have supported and participated in methods of conditioning that lead to a progressive weakening of the victims' physical capacities, and in the savage use of psychological or psychiatric methods designed to brainwash the cult members and place them in a condition of dependency.

The confirmed or potential danger of certain cults, with the presence and even the active cooperation of doctors in their midst, poses an acute moral and ethical problem with deontological overtones that reflects onto the entire medical profession.

The medical practices that show up inside the cult phenomena are very complex, especially given:

> - the extreme polymorphism of cults;
> - the very diverse degrees of participation of doctors in certain activities of cults;
> - the intricate blend of the various forms of collusion with cult movements of which a practitioner: might be guilty: a doctor may "recruit" his clients, and may also lend a hand to the "medical" activities of the cult, he may be an accessory to the illegal practice of medicine or provide a cover, claiming to be unaware of harmful, even dangerous practices.

Every time a doctor is reported for any type of cult-related abnormality, an objective analysis of the circumstances and the evidence is essential; and once the facts have been gathered and assessed, there must be consequences imposed by the public health authorities.

The European principles of medical ethics, adopted in 1987, also stipulate: "The doctor shall avoid imposing upon the patient his personal philosophical, moral or political opinions in the practice of his profession"; thus, any proselytism in favor of cult movements in the scope of the medical practice is banned.

Sanctions Against Fake Medical Practices

In a recent hearing in France, the cult IVI and the doctors who collaborated in its practices were tried and convicted, and one doctor was barred for life from any further practice of medicine. Dr. X was convicted of having disregarded the basic medical principles and allowing one of his patients' cancer to progress, causing his death. In its decision, the National Council of Physicians gives an opinion that soft-pedals the hazards of homeopathy and the respect that certain experts accord it. Let us pray that in the future, the authorities will not shrink from confronting the storm that will be raised by lawsuits brought against these practitioners who are more charlatans than doctors.

To Conclude: The Pill for Fools

In another of its efforts to protect the public from moronic scams, the magazine *Science et Vie* published an article entitled "The Enigmatic Pill from the Kremlin", debunking one of the new fantasy products offered to gullible clients of the alternative medicine movement, in May 1997.

The Politburo pill, as it was called, was one of the by-products of the former USSR's military research and production. Invented at the Tomsk military-industrial complex, it seems that the Kremlin pill was intended for members of the Politburo and was supposed to have been used to treat the former First Party Secretary Leonid Brezhnev for gastric disorders. It was composed of a stainless steel case containing a silver oxide battery and a miniaturized electronic circuit that would emit discharges of approximately 20 millivolts under ten milliamperes. In 1985 and again in 1995 the pill received approval from the Soviet Ministry of Health. With the fall of the Soviet empire and the ensuing economic debacle, it was decided to offer this miracle pill — which had been kept under wraps and hidden as securely as a nuclear warhead — for sale on the international market.

The pill is relatively simple to use, except in the first phase, i.e. at the time of its ingestion. It's big: almost an inch long and a third of an inch wide. Once it has been swallowed and enters the acid environment of the stomach, the capsule behaves like an electro-stimulation system, producing mild electric shocks to the stomach wall for about 24 hours. This gastric system electric shock is recommended for various disorders: slow bowel, constipation, ulcers, stress, diabetes and migraine. But the magic pill can also be introduced into the vagina and used to treat cysts in the uterus. A Western medical-gadgets company was dreaming of importing and marketing the magic capsule, and there is no doubt that they would come up with testimonies of miraculous healings to bolster sales.

Big money is being made in the medical products and gadgetry market, and the possibilities are inexhaustible. From the "Hopi candle" promoted for cleaning the ears to the "Spina cushion" to straighten the spine, from the "magnetized funnel" for treating drinking water to the "protective magnetic-wave blanket", the market is immense. But maybe integral health with energy harmonization, or preparing bio-telluric meals, would be more your style? Then you can take part in introductory courses and learn all about them. Fear not, frauds and charlatans of all sorts are elbowing each other on their way to your door, to offer you products that will make you beautiful and healthy, tomorrow (maybe), but which will definitely make them rich today.

Don't hesitate, the field of medicine is still vast and unexplored, and your questions, even if they are numerous, will all be answered if you take enough courses. But don't ask too much — don't expect the answers to be logical. The principles of patamedicine don't hold water any better than a sieve.

Notes

Chapter 1.

1.   Iridology is a practice by which diagnoses are offered on the basis of an examination of the iris of one's eye.

2.   Trichology: a diagnostic technique based on the hair on one's body or one's head.

3.   LAPLANTINE, François and RABEYR, Paul-Louis, *Les Médecines parallèles*, PUF, "Que sais-je", 1987.

4.   SOURNIA, Jean-Charles, "Introduction aux médecines non expérimentales", *Science et vie*, n° 150, March 1985.

5.   ILLICH, Ivan, *La Convivialité*, Seuil, 1972; *Libérer l'avenir*, Seuil, 1971; *Némésis médicale*, Seuil, 1981.

6.   See *infra* p. 144 and the following.

7.   See LAPLANTINE, François and RABEYR, Paul-Louis, *Les Médecines parallèles*, *op. cit.*

8.   Centrotherapy aims to create physiological responses by stimulating different points of the nasal lining by touching or pricking it.

9.   See WEISZ, Georges, "Un temps fort, la crise des années trente", *La Recherche*, dossier sur l'homéopathie, n° 310, June 1998.

Chapter 2.

1.   1,400 doctors are practicing homeopathy, according to the French National Health Insurance Bureau, and some 3,000 say their practice is "homeopathically oriented" according to the National Union of French Homeopathic Doctors.

2.   The homeopathic industry is dominated, on the world market, by two French companies, Boiron and Dolisos (which was recently acquired by the Pierre

Fabre group). Quoted on the secondary stock exchange, Boiron, the world leader, showed a turnover of 1.25 billion francs in 1996 (of which some 312 million were made in foreign markets) and net revenues of 76.6 million. The group's turnover went up that year by 12% in the United States, 21% in Canada, 13% in Spain and 10% in Italy. Dolisos reported a turnover of 600 million francs in 1996. The third largest producer, worldwide, is the German company Heel. According to Peter Fisher, the market has gone up by 15% annually in the U.S. and Great Britain. The world market is estimated at 6 billion francs, with France accounting for 30% of that and North America for 20% (*La Recherche*, n° 310, June 1998).

3. Quoted in ROUZÉ, Michel, "Pour ou contre l'homéopathie", *Science et vie*, n° 807, December 1984, p. 48-55.

4. The d'Avogadro number is the number of molecules present in one mole of a pure substance. It is on the order of 10^{23}. A homeopathic medication at a dilution of 30 H C has been diluted to 1.10^{-60} of the original substance. From 12 H C (Hahnemannian centesimals) or 23 H D (Hahnemannian decimals) on up, it is likely that a dose of the medication might not have a single molecule of the product in question. Tests conducted on high dilutions, such as those by Benveniste, have met the limits of ultramolecular chemistry. At this level, agents of contamination such as silica from the glass laboratory equipment occur in greater quantities than the product being tested.

5. See "L'homéopathie au banc d'essai", *La Recherche*, n° 310, June 1998.

6. ROSSION, Pierre, "Villeneuve d'Ascq. Le Tchernobyl homéopathique aurait pu être évité", *Science et vie*, n° 899, c 1992, p. 54-57.

7. Cited in *Science et vie*, n° 807, December 1984.

8. See "L'homéopathie au banc d'essai", *op. cit.*

9. This article from *Nature* had been reprinted the year before in n° 135 of *The European Journal of Pharmacology*.

10. BROCH, Henri, *Au cœur de l'extraordinaire*, L'Horizon chimérique, 1994, p. 145-183. The degranulation test for basophiles: in subjects who are sensitive to a given allergen (allergic subjects), an abnormal elevation of antibodies belonging to the class of Immunoglobulin E is observed (IgE). These IgE characteristically attach themselves to certain receptor sites on the membrane of certain cells such as the white blood cells. These basophiles contain granules made up of two substances: one is an anticoagulant, the other is a histamine, a chemical mediator that is responsible for allergic reactions. The allergic reaction is represented by the union of one allergen and two IgE's on the cell wall of the baso-

philes. This reaction is accompanied by an increase of histamines in the blood, and releases the anticoagulant factor. The degranulation test is intended to demonstrate a change in the coloration of the granules of the basophiles under the influence of an allergen (on goat's Anti-IgE, in Benveniste's experiments). When the basophiles "degranulate", they release the histamine, signaling an allergic reaction, and they lose their color. Now, a decoloration or achromasy may be observed even without its being the result of degranulation — which seems to have been the case in Benveniste's experiments (unless fraud may have been a factor). Real degranulation as a reaction should allow for the histamine to be found in the solution (which was not the case in Benveniste's tests).

11. MESSADIÉ, Gérald, "Et la mémoire des gaz?", *Science et vie*, n° 852, September 1988.

12. ROSSION, Pierre, "Homéopathie, la mystification recommence", *Science et vie*, n° 955, April 1997, p. 77-85.

13. ROSSION, Pierre, "La vérité sur la mémoire de l'eau", *Science et vie*, n° 850, August 1988, p. 10-19.

14. See BROCH, Henri, *Au cœur de l'extraordinaire, op. cit.*

15. *Ibid.*,Quoting *L'Homéopathie. Approche historique et critique*, by J. Jacques AULAS (Paris, 1985).

16. Pathogenesis: the start of a somatic process that is masked as a disease, with or without any real basis of pathology existing.

17. BROCH, Henri, *Au cœur de l'extraordinaire, op. cit.*, p. 151-152.

18. A dilution procedure, dreamed up by one Korsakov, simpler than the Hahnemann process because successive dilutions are made in one single flask. But this method cannot assure the desired regular deconcentration. Korsakov's principle of dilution was banned in France until, in order to satisfy the requirements for standardization throughout Europe, it was reintroduced under a directive from the European Community on September 22, 1992.

19. *La Recherche*, n° 310, June 1998.

20. Despite repeated opposition from the Commission on Transparency, 1163 homeopathic medications are 65% reimbursable, a rate that is supposed, in principle, to be reserved for products that have been proven effective against problems of a certain degree of severity. It is hard to assess how much harm has been done by the national medical authorities that decide on these products, given that an adequate coding system is lacking. The Syndicate of the Homeopathic Industry estimates it at 1.2% (and certain others estimate 2%) of the total cost, overall, of medical reimbursements (Source: *La Recherche*, n° 310, June 1998).

Chapter 3.

1. AULAS, Jean-Jacques, *Les Médecines douces, des illusions qui guérissent, op. cit.*

2. SAGNIÈRES, Claire, "L'acupuncture. Mythes et réalité", *Médecine et Hygiène*, 1989.

3. The great heat source, or triple heater, has to do with the respiratory, digestive and genital organs in a vision of energy relations.

4. BEAU, Georges, *La Médecine chinoise*, Seuil, 1965.

5. VIBES, Jean, "La physique de l'acupuncture", *Aesculape*, n° 2, Sept.- Oct. 1996.

6. Bader, Jean-Michel, "Des acupuncteurs piqués au vif", *Science et vie*, n° 823, April 1986.

7. BROCH, Henri, *Au cœur de l'extraordinaire, op. cit.*

Chapter 4.

1. PIGANIOL Guy et coll., *Les Manipulations vertébrales*, GEMAFBC, Dijon, 1988.

2. *Ibid.*

3. PIGANIOL Guy, "Pratique des manipulations vertébrales; risques et accidents; aspects médico-légaux", *Revue française du dommage corporel*, tome XVI, n° 2, 1990.

4. HAMELIN, Jean-Pierre, "L'ostéopathie crânienne", *Le Médecin de Vendée*, July 1994.

5. Publicity brochure, s.d., s.l.

6. *Idem.*

7. The bulk of the experimental works that have tried to lend credit to the idea that the left brain governs reason and the right brain governs desire, the passions and emotions, relate to the study on neuropsychological behavior of patients with brain lesions — whether due to accidents or to major surgery. When the corpus callosum (which links the two hemispheres) is severed, it creates two individual and independent halves. Besides the fact that these tests studied a small number of subjects, with pathological problems, we cannot extrapolate the results to subjects with intact brains. On this topic, Prof. Lucien Israël's book *Cerveau droit-cerveau gauche*, from Éditions Plon, is useful.

8. Publicity brochure, s.d., s.l.

9. *Idem.*

10. *Idem.*

Chapter 5.

1. Excerpt from the *Petit Précis d'humanisme biologique*, Cited in PLUCHET, Régis, "La naturopathie c'est quoi au juste", *L'Impatient*, n° 26, 1976.

2. Cited in *L'Impatient*, n° 26, 1976.

3. "Qu'est-ce que la naturopathie?", publicity brochure from a naturopath, s.d., s.l.

4. In 1848, Arnold Rickli founded the first sanatorium where sun and air baths were practiced.

5. Cited in *L'Impatient*.

6. Cited in *L'Impatient*.

7. "La naturothérapie dentaire", *Revue internationale des médecines non conventionnelles*, n° 2, Sept.-Oct. 1996.

8. MONNIER, Georges, "Pour se désintoxiquer, l'hydrothérapie du côlon" (from a photocopy distributed at a conference, undated).

Chapter 6.

1. One of the better known books in the literature of alchemy.

2. See "La logique du vivant", *L'Impatient*, n° 152-153, July-August 1990.

Chapter 7.

1. ELIADE, Mircea, *Histoire des croyances et idées religieuses*, Payot, 1976.

2. LEPAROUX, Gérard, "L'iridologie", *Le Médecin de Vendée*, July 1994.

3. JAUSAS, Gilbert, *Traité pratique d'iridologie médicale*, Éditions Dangles, 1983.

4. *Ibid.*

5. BROCH, Henri, *Au cœur de l'extraordinaire*, *op. cit.*

Chapter 8.

1. Publicity brochure, s.d., s.l.

2. See *Pouvoir occulte des pierres précieuses*, Desforges, 1968.

Chapter 9.

1. RAVSKY, Franklin, *Mesmer ou la Révolution thérapeutique*, Payot, 1977.

2. *Ibid.*

3. ROCARD, Yves, *Les Sourciers*, PUF, 1982.

4. DADOUN, Roger, *Cent Fleurs pour Wilhelm Reich*, Payot, "Petite Bibliothèque", 1975.

5. See REICH, Wilhelm, *La Biopathie du cancer* (1948), Payot, 1975.

6. This and the following citations in the subchapter are excerpted from a tract published by a geobiologist.

7. ESCANDE, Jean-Paul, *Mirages de la médecine*, Albin Michel, 1987.

Chapter 10.

1. See *infra* p. 144 and after, "L'affaire Beljanski".

2. LARGER, Jean, "À propos d'un cas de cancer du sinus piriforme traité par les péroxydases oléiques", *Annales d'oto-rhino-laryngologie*, 1956, p. 353.

3. See ROSSION, Pierre, "Beljanski: génie ou charlatan", *Science et vie*, n° 914, November 1993.

4. See "Un médicament étouffé", *L'Impatient*, n° 73, December 1983.

Chapter 11.

1. ROUZÉ, Michel, "La mystique biologico-marine", *Science et vie*, n° 875, August 1990.

2. *Ibid.*

3. MARTINEZ GARCIA, Francisco et CAMOV, Isabel, "Les traumatismes de la naissance", *Incroyable et scientifique*, n° 4, 2nd trimester 1995.

4. *Ibid.*

5. *Le Parisien libéré*, December 21, 1995.

6. *L'Express*, March 21, 996.

Chapter 12.

1. KLEIN, Bernard, "L'approche spirituelle de la dépression", *Vie naturelle*, n° 124, February 1997.

Chapter 13.

1. Gnostic Association of Anthropologic and Cultural Studies.

2. Tantric Yoga: yoga founded upon the awakening of sexual energy and kundalini, with a progressive increase in the energy from the sacro-coccygian

chakra up to the occipital chakra; this awakening of energy is construed as being synonymous with progressive enlightenment.

3. *Le travail erroné des cinq centres*, a document from AGÉAC.

4. *Arcane AZF*, a document from AGÉAC.

5. *Le foie...*, a document from AGÉAC.

6. The quotations on these pages are taken from internal documents from AGÉAC.

7. CCMM (Comité de documentation, d'éducation et d'action contre les manipulations mentales), *Les Sectes. État d'urgence*, Albin Michel, 1995.

8. "Seikai Mahikari Bunmei Kyodan ou la Lumière des miracles", an internal document.

9. *Idem.*

10. *Idem.* Ken = perfect health, Wa = harmony, Fu = wealth.

11. Internal document from Mahikari quoted in *Les Sectes. États d'urgence, op. cit.*

12. Elementary initiatory course in Mahikari, internal document.

13. See *Les Sectes. États d'urgence, op. cit.* The quotations in the rest of this subchapter are from the same source.

14. LANCTÔT, Ghislaine, *La Mafia médicale*, Voici la Clef, Québec, 1993.

15. *Le Journal de Montréal*, August 23, 1995.

16. *Le Journal de Montréal*, August 29, 1995.

17. *Midi libre*, November 16, 1996.

18. *Ibid.*

19. *La Dépêche du Midi*, January 23, 1996; *Midi libre*, November 16, 1996.

20. *Panorama du Médecin*, n° 3591, April 29, 1992.

21. See BAUDET, Cécile, "Enquête sur l'Énergo-chromo-kinèse", *L'Impatient*, n° 171, February 1992.

22. *Panorama du médecin*, n° 3591, April 29, 1992.

23. *Panorama du médecin*, n° 3589, April 27, 1992. See also "Les pilules dorées du bon docteur Vévet", *Challenges*, January 1993.

24. Remarks by Dr. Jean Brudon, President of the National Order of Pharmacists, *Panorama du médecin*, n° 3591, April 29, 1992.

25. Internal document from ÉCK.

26. HAMER, Rike Geed, *Fondement d'une médecine nouvelle*, Éditions ASAC, Chambéry, 1988.

27. MICHELINI, Hélène, "Enquête sur la méthode Hamer", *L'Impatient*, n° 170, January 1992.

28. *Cf. La Voix de l'Aisne*, December 22, 1996, January 26 and October 30, 1997; *L'Aisne nouvelle*, June 17, 1997.

29. *Les Sectes. États d'urgence, op. cit.*

30. ABGRALL, Jean-Marie, *La Mécanique des sectes*, Payot, 1996.

Chapter 14.

1. Cited in ESCANDE, Jean-Paul, *Mirages de la médecine, op. cit.* p. 215-216.

2. Statements from the Congress of the Association Life and Action, November 1993.

3. *Vie et action*, n° 201, May - June 1994.

4. *Idem.*

5. *Idem.*

6. "L'éternel présent", 4th broadcast.

7. Excerpts from the "Système du corps-miroir", internal document.

8. *Idem.*

9. THORWALD, Jurgen, *Histoire de la médecine dans l'Antiquité*, Hachette, 1962.

10. Leaflet from the "union" Hippocrate (President: Dr Alain Scohy).

11. *Idem.*

12. BASTIDE, Roger, from the article "Magie" in *Encyclopaedia Universalis*.

13. MAUSS, Marcel, *Mélange d'histoire des religions*, Paris, 1909.

14. MICHAUD, Jacques, *Médecines ésotériques, médecines de demain*, Denoël, 1976.

Also from Algora Publishing:

CLAUDIU A. SECARA
THE NEW COMMONWEALTH
From Bureaucratic Corporatism to Socialist Capitalism

The notion of an elite-driven worldwide perestroika has gained some credibility lately. The book examines in a historical perspective the most intriguing dialectic in the Soviet Union's "collapse" — from socialism to capitalism and back to socialist capitalism — and speculates on the global implications.

IGNACIO RAMONET
THE GEOPOLITICS OF CHAOS

The author, Director of Le Monde Diplomatique, presents an original, discriminating and lucid political matrix for understanding what he calls the "current disorder of the world" in terms of Internationalization, Cyberculture and Political Chaos.

TZVETAN TODOROV
A PASSION FOR DEMOCRACY –
Benjamin Constant

The French Revolution rang the death knell not only for a form of society, but also for a way of feeling and of living; and it is still not clear as yet what did we gain from the changes.

MICHEL PINÇON & MONIQUE PINÇON-CHARLOT
GRAND FORTUNES –
Dynasties of Wealth in France

Going back for generations, the fortunes of great families consist of far more than money—they are also symbols of culture and social interaction. In a nation known for democracy and meritocracy, piercing the secrets of the grand fortunes verges on a crime of lèse-majesté . . . Grand Fortunes succeeds at that.

CLAUDIU A. SECARA
TIME & EGO –
Judeo-Christian Egotheism and the Anglo-Saxon Industrial Revolution

The first question of abstract reflection that arouses controversy is the problem of Becoming. Being persists, beings constantly change; they are born and they pass away. How can Being change and yet be eternal? The quest for the logical and experimental answer has just taken off.

JEAN-MARIE ABGRALL
SOUL SNATCHERS: THE MECHANICS OF CULTS

Jean-Marie Abgrall, psychiatrist, criminologist, expert witness to the French Court of Appeals, and member of the Inter-Ministry Committee on Cults, is one of the experts most frequently consulted by the European judicial and legislative processes. The fruit of fifteen years of research, his book delivers the first methodical analysis of the sectarian phenomenon, decoding the mental manipulation on behalf of mystified observers as well as victims.

JEAN-CLAUDE GUILLEBAUD

THE TYRANNY OF PLEASURE

Guillebaud, a Sixties' radical, re-thinks liberation, taking a hard look at the question of sexual morals -- that is, the place of the forbidden -- in a modern society. For almost a whole generation, we have lived in the illusion that this question had ceased to exist. Today the illusion is faded, but a strange and tumultuous distress replaces it. No longer knowing very clearly where we stand, our societies painfully seek answers between unacceptable alternatives: bold-faced permissiveness or nostalgic moralism.

SOPHIE COIGNARD AND MARIE-THÉRÈSE GUICHARD

FRENCH CONNECTIONS –
The Secret History of Networks of Influence

They were born in the same region, went to the same schools, fought the same fights and made the same mistakes in youth. They share the same morals, the same fantasies of success and the same taste for money. They act behind the scenes to help each other, boosting careers, monopolizing business and information, making money, conspiring and, why not, becoming Presidents!

VLADIMIR PLOUGIN

RUSSIAN INTELLIGENCE SERVICES. Vol. I. Early Years

Mysterious episodes from Russia's past – alliances and betrayals, espionage and military feats – are unearthed and examined in this study, which is drawn from ancient chronicles and preserved documents from Russia, Greece, Byzantium and the Vatican Library. Scholarly analysis and narrative flair combine to give both the fact and the flavor of the battle scenes and the espionage milieu, including the establishment of secret services in Kievan rus, the heroes and the techniques of intelligence and counter-intelligence in the 10th-12th centuries, and the times of Vladimir.

JEAN-JACQUES ROSA

EURO ERROR

The European Superstate makes Jean-Jacques Rosa mad, for two reasons. First, actions taken to relieve unemployment have created inflation, but have not reduced unemployment. His second argument is even more intriguing: the 21st century will see the fragmentation of the U. S., not the unification of Europe.

ANDRÉ GAURON

EUROPEAN MISUNDERSTANDING

Few of the books decrying the European Monetary Union raise the level of the discussion to a higher plane. European Misunderstanding is one of these. Gauron gets it right, observing that the real problem facing Europe is its political future, not its economic future.

DOMINIQUE FERNANDEZ

PHOTOGRAPHER: FERRANTE FERRANTI

ROMANIAN RHAPSODY — An Overlooked Corner of Europe

"Romania doesn't get very good press." And so, renowned French travel writer Dominique Fernandez and top photographer Ferrante Ferranti head out to form their own images. In four long journeys over a 6-year span, they uncover a tantalizing blend of German efficiency and Latin nonchalance, French literature and Gypsy music, Western rationalism and Oriental mysteries. Fernandez reveals the rich Romanian essence. Attentive and precise, he digs beneath the somber heritage of communism to reach the deep roots of a European country that is so little-known.

PHILIPPE TRÉTIACK

ARE YOU AGITÉ? Treatise on Everyday Agitation

"A book filled with the exuberance of a new millennium, full of humor and relevance. Philippe Trétiack, a leading reporter for Elle, goes around the world and back, taking an interest in the futile as well as the essential. His flair for words, his undeniable culture, help us to catch on the fly what we really are: characters subject to the ballistic impulse of desires, fads and a click of the remote. His book invites us to take a healthy break from the breathless agitation in general." — Aujourd'hui le Parisien

The 'Agité,' that human species that lives in international airports, jumps into taxis while dialing the cell phone, eats while clearing the table, reads the paper while watching TV and works during vacation – has just been given a new title." — Le Monde des Livres

PAUL LOMBARD

VICE & VIRTUE — Men of History, Great Crooks for the Greater Good

Personal passion has often guided powerful people more than the public interest. With what result? From the courtiers of Versailles to the back halls of Mitterrand's government, from Danton — revealed to have been a paid agent for England — to the shady bankers of Mitterrand's era, from the buddies of Mazarin to the builders of the Panama Canal, Paul Lombard unearths the secrets of the corridors of power. He reveals the vanity and the corruption, but also the grandeur and panache that characterize the great. This cavalcade over many centuries can be read as a subversive tract on how to lead.

RICHARD LABÉVIÈRE

DOLLARS FOR TERROR — The U.S. and Islam

"In this riveting, often shocking analysis, the U.S. is an accessory in the rise of Islam, because it manipulates and aids radical Moslem groups in its shortsighted pursuit of its economic interests, especially the energy resources of the Middle East and the oil- and mineral-rich former Soviet republics of Central Asia. Labévière shows how radical Islamic fundamentalism spreads its influence on two levels, above board, through investment firms, banks and shell companies, and clandestinely, though a network of drug dealing, weapons smuggling and money laundering. This important book sounds a wake-up call to U.S. policy-makers." — Publishers Weekly

Jeannine Verdès-Leroux

DECONSTRUCTING PIERRE BOURDIEU

Against Sociological Terrorism From the Left

Sociologist Pierre Bourdieu went from widely-criticized to widely-acclaimed, without adjusting his hastily constructed theories. Turning the guns of critical analysis on his own critics, he was happier jousting in the ring of (often quite undemocratic) political debate than reflecting and expanding upon his own propositions. Verdès-Leroux has spent 20 years researching the policy impact of intellectuals who play at the fringes of politics. She suggests that Bourdieu arrogated for himself the role of "total intellectual" and proved that a good offense is the best defense. A pessimistic Leninist bolstered by a ponderous scientific construct, Bourdieu stands out as the ultimate doctrinaire more concerned with self-promotion than with democratic intellectual engagements.

Henri Troyat

TERRIBLE TZARINAS

Who should succeed Peter the Great? Upon the death of this visionary and despotic reformer, the great families plotted to come up with a successor who would surpass everyone else — or at least, offend none. But there were only women — Catherine I, Anna Ivanovna, Anna Leopoldovna, Elizabeth I. These autocrats imposed their violent and dissolute natures upon the empire, along with their loves, their feuds, their cruelties. Born in 1911 in Moscow, Troyat is a member of the Académie française, recipient of Prix Goncourt.

Jean-Marie Abgrall

HEALING OR STEALING — Medical Charlatans in the New Age

Jean-Marie Abgrall is Europe's foremost expert on cults and forensic medicine. He asks, are fear of illness and death the only reasons why people trust their fates to the wizards of the pseudo-revolutionary and the practitioners of pseudo-magic? We live in a bazaar of the bizarre, where everyday denial of rationality has turned many patients into ecstatic fools. While not all systems of nontraditional medicine are linked to cults, this is one of the surest avenues of recruitment, and the crisis of the modern world may be leading to a new mystique of medicine where patients check their powers of judgment at the door.

Dr. Deborah Schurman-Kauflin

THE NEW PREDATOR: WOMEN WHO KILL — Profiles of Female Serial Killers

This is the first book ever based on face-to-face interviews with women serial killers.

Rémi Kauffer

DISINFORMATION — US Multinationals at War with Europe

"Spreading rumors to damage a competitor, using 'tourists' for industrial espionage. . . Kauffer shows how the economic war is waged." — *Le Monde*

"A specialist in the secret services, he notes, 'In the era of CNN, with our skies full of satellites and the Internet expanding every nano-second, the techniques of mass persuasion that were developed during the Cold War are still very much in use – only their field of application has changed.' His analysis is shocking, and well-documented." — *La Tribune*